The Walls Came Tumbling Down

Un Film de Robert Anton Wilson

Other Titles From New Falcon Publications

Reality Is What You Can Get Away With
The Cosmic Trigger series (Volumes I, II and III)
    By Robert Anton Wilson
Undoing Yourself With Energized Meditation
Sex Magic, Tantra & Tarot: The Way of the Secret Lover
    By Christopher S. Hyatt, Ph.D.
Rebels & Devils: The Psychology of Liberation
    Edited by C. S. Hyatt, contributions by Wm. S. Burroughs et al.
Urban Voodoo: A Beginner's Guide to Afro-Caribbean Magic
Pacts With the Devil: A Chronicle of Sex, Blasphemy & Liberation
    By S. Jason Black and Christopher. S. Hyatt, Ph.D.
Eight Lectures on Yoga
The Law Is For All
Magick Without Tears
    By Aleister Crowley
The Intelligence Agents
Neuropolitique
The Game of Life
    By Timothy Leary, Ph.D.
PsyberMagick: Advanced Ideas in Chaos Magick
    By Peter J. Carroll
Zen Without Zen Masters
    By Camden Benares
The Complete Golden Dawn System of Magic
    By Israel Regardie
Astrology & Consciousness
    By Rio Olesky
A Soul's Journey: Whispers From the Light
    By Patricia Idol
Breaking the Illusion: Tools for Self-Awakening
    By Ric Weinman
Spirit & Matter: New Horizons for Medicine
    By José Lacerda de Azevedo, M.D.
Conversations With My Dark Side
    By Shanti Ananda
Reclaiming the Dark Feminine: The Price of Desire
    By Carolyn Baker, Ph.D.

And to get your free catalog of *all* of our titles, write to:

NEW FALCON PUBLICATIONS
Catalog Dept.
1739 East Broadway Road, Suite 1-277
Tempe, AZ 85282 U.S.A.

Robert
Anton
Wilson

THE
WALLS
CAME
TUMBLING
DOWN

NEW FALCON PUBLICATIONS

International Standard Book Number: 0-56184-091-2
Library of Congress Catalog Card Number: 96-68643

First Edition 1997

The paper used in this publication meets the minimum requirements of the American National Standard for Permanence of Paper for Printed Library Materials Z39.48-1984

Address all inquiries to:
NEW FALCON PUBLICATIONS
1739 East Broadway Road Suite 1-277
Tempe, AZ 85282 U.S.A.
(or)
1209 South Casino Center.
Las Vegas, NV 89104 U.S.A.

Contents

Introduction

No two equals are the same.
— Malaclypse the Younger,
Principia Discordia

I wrote the screenplay for *The Walls Came Tumbling Down* in 1988 or 1989 in West Los Angeles after one film deal had gone down the toilet and while I tried to get another deal together. I loved the L.A. area in those days, and all criticism of "LaLa Land" seemed to me based on ignorant snobbery and envy. After six years in Ireland, where the year consists of "nine months of winter and three months of ungodly weather" as the Dublin adage[1] says, the Southern California climate seemed like the Garden of Eden, and I met a lot of wonderful, intelligent people, along with the usual atavistic hominids you meet everywhere in any city. It took a while to notice the extent of the smog (on many sunny

---

[1] Dublin days come in three types: soft days, hearty days, and filthy days. Soft days have light, gentle rain; hearty days, heavy rain and some wind; filthy days, heavier rain and violent wind. As one grizzled Dubliner said to another, "Terrible weather for this time of year, Paddy." Paddy replied sadly, "Ah, sure, it isn't this time of year at all, at all."

days you don't see it at all—not in West L.A., anyway).
When the smog became impossible to ignore and bur-
glaries had occurred in the house on our right *and* also
in the house at our left, I decided I couldn't stand any
large American city anymore and moved to the Santa
Cruz mountains. (Similar exacerbations of pollution
and crime had previously driven me out of New York,
Chicago and San Francisco.)

In the warm green time when I still loved L.A. and
wrote this script, I called the screenplay *The Man Who
Murdered God,* a slight case of self-plagiarism (since I
had already used that title for one chapter in *Illumina-
tus!*). I think the new title fits better. It intends to invoke
not only the walls of Jericho in the Bible fable—which
came tumbling down in an instant, in the blink of an
eye—but also the tunnel-walls of the labyrinth of Minos
in the Greek myth, which hid Theseus and the Monster
from each other for a long while before their final con-
frontation. These myths do not underlie this screenplay
to the extent that Homer's *Odyssey* underlies Joyce's
Ulysses, but they do have a strong umbilical link to my
story.

Of course, I also had in mind the walls of our individual reality-tunnels. The basic imagery of falling walls
and sudden defenselessness or revelation resonates sym-
bolically (at least in my mind) to the famous Zen *koan*:

"What is the Buddha-mind?"
"The bottom falling out of the bucket."

I suppose you have to visualize the bucket as full of
water to "get" the imagistic joke here—or maybe you
just have to remember the very best orgasm of your
entire life......

As intelligent readers will quickly realize, this script deals with the scary things that happen to those who stumble into this borderless or other-worldly consciousness without any intent to go there and without any preparation or Operating Manual to tell them how to navigate when the walls tumble, the doors of perception fly open and the bottom falls out of their mental filing cabinet, leaving the brain suddenly free of the limits of "mind." This topic appears, one way or another, in most of my fiction, because it seems to me one of the most important and most ignored social facts of our time. For various reasons we live in an age when boundary walls of all sorts—neurological, sexual, conceptual, nationalistic, ideological—have started falling without warning on the heads of people who never expected such things to happen to them.

If magick and mysticism signify conscious efforts to break down the conditioned/imprinted "maps" (territorial imperatives of "mind") in our brains, the world-round UFO experience, and many similar nonordinary perceptions, represent the boundaries or Berlin Walls vanishing suddenly for people who have not in any way desired or sought such mind-bending events, which always feel, to some extent, like walking from one room to another in your own house and finding yourself in the middle of St. John's Apocalypse—with the Marx Brothers as the Four Horsemen.

To clarify the above: when I use the term *brain* I mean to signify not only the organ in our heads but all the neural circuits that feed thereto, and their links with other systems, e.g., the neuro-endocrine circuits, neuro-immunological circuits, etc.; the whole of what some scientists now call the brainbody. When I use the word "*mind*" (always in quotes) I mean to designate the imprinted-conditioned neurolinguistic grid that makes up our individual reality-tunnel, i.e., the type of self-hypnosis we find most congenial. (For further light, see my *Prometheus Rising*, Dr. Timothy Leary's *Info-Psychology*, or the writings of Dr. Richard Bandler on neuro-linguistic programming.)

Michael Ellis, the "hero" of my story, owes his name to a classic Monty Python routine, but finds himself stranded between a Pythonesque world and an Ed Wood/tabloid/*X-Files* nightmare. Since several million Americans still find themselves lost in that neurological Area 51 (not to mention the millions more elsewhere on the planet), I think we should try to understand what has happened to the human race in the last few decades of this century.

Several surveys have measured the extent to which the "unthinkable" has entered the experience of modern humanity; I will not bother quoting any of them here, since almost everybody knows the general picture. Despite all the Establishment says, the fastest-growing minority on the planet consists of those who have already experienced High Weirdness—"telepathy," UFO abductions, impossible memories, "out of body experiences," recollections of "past lives," etc. Whether one thinks of such experiences as occurring in conventional space-time or in some nonordinary neuro-space, they keep on happening, to more and more of us.

Any "proof" (or attempted "proof") that these things do not happen in conventional space-time does not help or enlighten the persons who have had these experiences and want to know what the hell it all means. If really convinced that their experience did not occur in consensus reality, these people will want to know what other kind of reality they wandered into, and lacking rational models for this sort of human experience, they will perforce seize on some fashionable but irrational model.

Scientists who worry about the growing popularity of such irrational models or Belief Systems (B.S.)[1] should realize that until they offer better B.S. the most popular kinds of pre-or-non-scientific B.S. around will just get more popular every year. As I think I once wrote somewhere else, when science refuses to offer explanations or even to look at the data, the general public will simply choose among the various unscientific explanations available.

For instance, most of the really weird events in this story actually happened to people I have known. I don't venture an opinion here about what kind of brainspace they happened in, but they happened. Some of them happened to me, as readers of my *Cosmic Trigger I: Final Secret of the Illuminati* will realize; but most of them happened to other people. In every case, I only heard about the events after the persons involved knew me long enough to feel sure that I would not immediately classify them as "nuts." I sometimes think that, just as medieval people feared to discuss certain perceptions out of fear that everybody would call them "heretics," modern people fear to discuss the same sort of data out of fear that somebody will call them psycho. I suppose that linguistic reform represents progress of some sort, but I don't feel sure *what* sort. The authorities burned "heretics" at the stake, but the worst that

---

[1] I owe this delightful abbreviation to David Jay Brown, author of *Brainchild* (New Falcon Publications, 1989).

happens to "psychotics" nowadays will probably consist of over-medication.

THANKS FOR
THE MEMORIES

Doubt everything.
—Frater Perdurabo, *The Book of Lies*

The first time I saw a "flying saucer" happened in Brooklyn during the first wave of "saucer" excitement during the summer of 1947 or '48. My parents and I, sitting on our verandah, saw the "saucer" cross the sky, rather slowly, and watched for about three minutes before the taller buildings downtown blocked it from our view. At the age of 15 or 16 I found this tremendously thrilling and wanted to make it even more thrilling by reporting it to the police or the *Brooklyn Eagle*. My parents absolutely refused to allow this, and said I should never even talk about it to my friends. I think I can best summarize their attitude as "People who see such things get laughed at, we don't want to get laughed at, so we will pretend we didn't see it."

Since we didn't report this, no investigation followed and I have no idea what the hell we saw that evening. A weather balloon? An airplane given a strange oval-like glint by the twilight? A real honest-to-gosh Space Ship? Swamp gas? A "heat inversion"? None of those labels seems absolutely convincing to me, at this stage, because I just don't have any data to judge by. All I know about the damned thing consists in the observations that it *looked* oval and it *seemed* to glint like a metal craft of some sort. Note that I do not say it "was" oval or "was" a metal craft; I report what I saw in a purely phenomenological manner.

(Frankly, the weather balloon theory seems most probable to me right now ... but I don't claim to *know*....)

I recall this story here only because it illustrates the conditioned reflexes of most of humanity throughout most of our history. When confronted with the mysterious, the inexplicable or the unsettling, popular wisdom tells us we should *ignore it and hope it will go away.* (An Irish proverb says, "If you see a two-headed pig, keep your mouth shut.") Just about the only humans not governed by this infophobic reflex have dwelt in the bohemian artistic and "deviant" sub-cultures, where the dominant attitude partakes more of infophilia. (As one of Shakespeare's characters says, "If it be new, it matters not how vile.")

I have made Mike Ellis a strongly infophobic type, and shown him unwillingly pushed toward infophilia, because I think of him as a sort of 20th Century Everyman, and modern experience, as it graduates into the postmodern, seems to have overwhelming tendencies to move more and more people from infophobia to infophilia, sometimes with shocking and traumatic abruptness.

Let me define the two key terms I have just used. As readers of *Prometheus Rising* will remember, the Leary model of "first circuit" (infantile, oral) consciousness has a forward-back polarity: we tend to go *forward* to Mother/safe-space or anything motherly (associated with mother/safety by genetic programs, imprints or conditioning) and we tend to retreat *backward* away from the unmotherly, the unsafe, the predatory. This level of consciousness exists throughout faunal evolution, and in humans it forms the bedrock of either an innovative/creative or a conservative/conformist lifestyle. In my first attempts to popularize Dr. Leary's work, I called these tendencies "*neophilia*" (creative) and "*neophobia*" (conformist). I have more recently decided that *infophilia* and *infophobia* have more generality and describe the associated reflexes more broadly.

The pure infophobe (represented not too badly by most "respectable" law-abiding citizens anywhere) obsessively avoids exotic foods, exotic ideas, exotic clothing, exotic people, "dern foreigners," new technology, innovative art or music, tabu subjects, originality, creativity, etc. Senator Exon, Senator Gramm, most of Congress, Theodore Roszack and Unabomber represent various styles of compulsive infophobic imprints.

The pure infophile remains a relatively rare person at this primitive stage of evolution. The infophile seeks out the new and exotic in food, ideas, clothing, technology, art—everywhere. Picasso, Joyce, Niels Bohr, Bucky Fuller and all the murdered heretics and innovators of history represent extreme infophiliac imprints.

In *Cosmic Trigger III: My Life After Death*, I represented these extremes by CSICOP (Committee for Scientific Investigation of Claims of the Paranormal), representing infophobia, and CSICON (Committee for Surrealist Investigation of Claims of the Normal) representing infophilia. Amusingly, many readers assumed I invented one of these organizations as a hoax or Swiftian satire, but they disagreed about *which* one....

Most of us, of course, exist somewhere on the continuum between pure infophobia and pure infophilia.

(Personally, I lean toward infophilia about almost everything except eating octopus, in which case I remain nervously infophobic. I tried it once, and only once. I'd rather try digesting the back left tire of my car.)

Unfortunately for the infophobic majority, civilization derives from increasingly rapid information processing, which means that those "open societies" which accumulate information fastest provide a higher quality of life in all respects than the "closed societies" where infophobia dominates.[1]

Tribal societies, where tabu imprisons the minds of its members in strict infophobia, never advance beyond Stone Age conditions until or unless incorporated into more "open" societies.

After the coming of the Holy Inquisition, nobody discovered any new chemical elements in the Catholic nations of Europe; all the new chemical discoveries, i.e., the majority of the elements now known, came from Protestant nations. (See my *Reality Is What You Can Get Away With* for more data on this.)

---

[1] The terms "open society" and "closed society" come from Sir Karl Popper's *The Open Society and Its Enemies*. Popper, as a scientist and as a horrified witness to the rise of Stalinist Communism and Nazism, regarded closed societies with even more alarm than I do (but his book makes an excellent polemic against all kinds of totalitarianism, including the kind that now reigns in our universities under the banner of Political Correctness). I feel that closed infophobic societies worked well enough to rank as evolutionary Relative Successes for most of human history; but I agree with Popper that they no longer work and that only open societies can serve humanity today.

Even today, the effects of the Inquisition linger on, visibly, in the quality of life in most of northern Europe as compared to southern (Catholic) Europe.

Similarly, seven years after the fall of the Soviet Union, the effects of the Stalinist closed society still hang on as a dead weight against the efforts of the reformers.

Moslem nations, although suddenly rich due to Oil, still show general backwardness compared to the more open European nations.

As Norbert Weiner, one of the first two mathematicians to define information[1] and show its importance, wrote once, "To live effectively is to live with adequate information." Infophobic societies do not live very well compared to more open societies where infophilia remains permissible even if not yet widespread. For instance, a United Nations study[2] of "quality of life," including education, life expectancy, civil liberties, medical care and economic wellbeing ranked the five top nations as:

> Canada
> Japan
> Iceland
> Sweden
> Switzerland

---

[1] Both Weiner and Claude Shannon came up with the basic equation at virtually the same time and each generously always insisted that the other deserved equal credit. Cf. Darwin and Wallace creating the theory of evolution by natural selection almost simultaneously, Newton and Leibnitz inventing calculus on nearly the same day, etc. This odd type of synchronicity deserves more study than it has received.

[2] Los Angeles *Times*, 23 May 1991.

None of these nations have one dominant religion or one dominant dogmatic ideology; all rank as "open" in Sir Karl Popper's sense, and all either encourage or allow infophilia. No Catholic or Islamic nation made it into the top five. Infophobia means stagnation and, usually, filth, poverty, plague and general misery. (And don't forget that what I here call infophobia means exactly what the Right Wing in this country calls "traditional family values," including the right to hate the same people that Grandpa hated.)

But an infophiliac age, such as we now willynilly live in, has its own risks, and the chief of these lies in the growing uncertainty that comes over all those who try to "keep up" with the latest discoveries. The most telling example of this social Uncertainty Principle: the dizzying attempt to find out what foods really nourish you and what foods might shorten your life. I sometimes think this adds a bit of stress to every mouthful of food we eat these days.

Every time a major new scientific study of nutrition and health appears, millions learn that some of what they have believed safe actually may contain hidden dangers—or, even weirder, foods considered dangerous by the known data of 1986 may look much safer according to the data of 1996. I use this example because more average persons try to keep up with this field than with any other; but the same general indefinite wobble infests all science lately.

If you have miraculously read enough to have the latest knowledge in all fields as of December 1996, a large part of what you know, or think you know, has already fallen under the axe of more recent research. But even more unsettlingly, you simply could not have read that much, even if you found a way to live without eating or sleeping. Dr. Stanley Ullam estimated, nearly 30 years ago, that the best-read full-time mathematicians knew about 5% of the theorems published since 1900; nobody in any other science knows much more than that about their own field. I once met a very knowledgeable physicist, who had specialized in rocketry and astronautics, and he not only knew less about Bell's Theorem than I, a layperson, did: he had actually never even heard of Bell's Theorem.

(I feel quite sure that among the 99% of biochemistry I know nothing about, there exist several discoveries as important as John Bell's nonlocality.)

If the polar caps melt, as in some doomsday scenarios, and our cities all sink below rising waves as Earth becomes all ocean, that will make a fit metaphor for the flood of information flowing through Internet and other modern electronic Media.

We all grow dizzy in this oceanic inundation of bytes, megabytes and gigabytes.

TRIAL BY FURY

"I'll be the judge, I'll by the jury,"
Said cunning old Fury,
"I'll hear the whole case
and condemn you to death."
—Lewis Carroll, *Alice in Wonderland*

Trial by jury goes back earlier than Athens, perhaps to Babylon (some say) but its modern, libertarian form we owe to some hard-headed pragmatic stubborn implacable barons who, in 1215 CE, hauled King John to an island called Runnymede on the Thames and wouldn't

let him go until he signed a document, now called
Magna Carta, which guaranteed, among other things,
that nobody could suffer for a criminal charge unless
the State could prove their case against him or her
beyond any reasonable doubt to a jury of twelve citizens of the realm.

Since Magna Carta the guarantee of trial of jury,
and the later guarantee that one would receive the treat-
ment due to an innocent person until such time as such
a jury ruled one guilty beyond a reasonable doubt, have
made the English legal system, and all systems deriva-
tive from it, the most admirable in the world. All the
major rebels against English imperialism kept that fea-
ture of the English system after throwing the English
themselves out. Trial by jury and presumption of inno-
cence form central parts of the radicalism of Jefferson
and Adams in America, Connolly and McBride in Ireland, the rebels in India and Kenya, and everywhere the
ideas of Magna Carta have reached.

All this now seems dead in the United States, due to
the O.J. Simpson case.

The Media, a contraption owned by a tiny handful
of elderly white males—a group that grows smaller
with each new "merger"—decided to pronounce Mr.
Simpson guilty the day after his arrest. Through all
their newspapers, radio shows, TV shows, etc., the
Media Moguls informed the public, day after day after
day, for months and months while the people who
would later become jurors would absorb all this lynchmob frenzy, that Simpson's guilt stood in a position of
Infallible Truth only equaled by the pronouncements of
the Vatican (and only equaled there in the minds of a
shrinking minority of overly-docile Catholics).

Somehow, the lynching mood did not infest a full
100% of the citizenry. Probably—or at least this theory
seems probable to me—the twelve on the jury balked
when perjury became overwhelmingly obvious in the
case of one of the two cops who collected the "evidence" against Simpson, and perjury seemed at least
probable in the case of the other cop. In any event, the
jury meditated, as law requires, and decided that the
State just had not proven Simpson guilty of anything,
beyond a reasonable doubt.

I don't see how they could have ruled otherwise.
With one proven perjurer and one probable perjurer as
major sources of "criminal evidence," that evidence
became worth zilch. Nothing in the State's case stood
"beyond a reasonable doubt" in such a travesty, especially since the perjurer had once confessed to planting
evidence whenever he needed to prove a case.

My intellect rebels against accepting anything from
such a witness, and the jurors also rebelled.

The Media refused to accept this rebellion, and this
spirit of independence, by the twelve jurors. Every day
the Media still bombard us—by print, radio and TV—
with insults to the uppity jurors who dared to follow
their oath and think for themselves. The same Media
also still carries endless reiterations of O.J. Simpson's
guilt. They now plot how to punish him, a difficult matter when dealing with a man declared not guilty under
American law, but they have decided to try starving him
out. A Media-organized boycott seems likely to drive
Simpson to the poor house or cause him to flee the
country.

Well, to look at the bright side, trial by jury still sur-
vives in England, Ireland, Scotland, Canada, Australia

and quite a few other places where the Magna Carta has more authority than the American Media.

In case this book lasts a century or more, let me explain that Mr. Simpson comes of African stock, at least partially. This bias and its associated contempt for due process couldn't have happened to a white man yet, despite the current megalomania of the Media. They haven't even treated President Clinton this viciously, or even President Roosevelt.

What has happened means that, in America, a jury's verdict of "not guilty" no longer frees an accused person of punishment. A Media verdict of guilty over-rules any jury verdict.

Such a total reversal of 781 years of Anglo-American law would have seemed impossible even as recently as two years ago.

The fact that "it only happened to a black man" gives small comfort to libertarians. Now that the Media knows its power, they can lynch *any defendent of any color* next time around.

And, if you don't see the relevance of the Simpson lynchmob to the major topic here, consider the following: in *Chaos and Beyond* (1994) I predicted, a bit whimsically, that the accelerating changes everywhere might lead to peace even in Northern Ireland. I felt rather awed by my own wisdom when the I.R.A. declared a cease-fire and began peace negotiations; I imagine some of my readers must have also considered me a pretty smart cookie to have foreseen such an unlikely event.

Now the I.R.A. have returned to war again and have set three bombs in London in the ten days before I sat down to write this page.

INTERESTING TIMES

Grrrrr!
—Robert Browning,
    "Soliloquy of the Spanish Cloister"

According to a legend I have always doubted, the Chinese have a curse which says, "May you live in intereresting times." I doubt this because you can't say that to anybody unless you live in the same times as they do; but nonetheless I find wisdom in the subtle Oriental irony here.

Nobody any longer doubts that we live in interesting times, or that they get more interesting every year.

If the Media has replaced the jury as arbiter of guilt in the U.S.A., the Palestinians, amazingly, have their own state again. And it exists, so far, in relative peace with its Israeli neighbors.

If the I.R.A. has given up negotiations and returned to bombs today, they may give up bombs and return to negotiations next Tuesday after lunch. Maybe.

Reports of UFOs, lake monsters, Bigfoot, etc. continue despite all Establishment denials.

The biggest event of the last decade—the collapse of the Soviet Union—occurred entirely without violence: the first nonviolent revolution of that size in *all* human history, extending from Berlin to Siberia.

Citizens of the U.S. now suffer the surrealist humiliation of urine testing on the job by our new Piss Police, a kind of totalitarian lunacy never dreamed of in the wildest satires of Kafka or Orwell.

Several universities now fund research on "near death" and "out of body" experiences.

Internet more and more evolves toward the "planetary brain" once only imagined by visionary scientists like Tielhard de Chardin and Arthur Clarke; and the U.S. Congress has panic attacks over the fact that some of this brain contains "pornographic" fantasy. (Do you know any brain that doesn't?)

A Japanese consortium plans to build a luxury hotel in outer space.

The most popular show on U.S. television, and now a big hit in England also, *The X-Files*, deals with governmental conspiracies that only the "kooks" took seriously a decade ago.

You've heard this already but *think* about it: Nelson Mandela has gone from a prison cell to the President's office in a country that has evolved from White Supremacy to power-sharing in only seven years.

We recently heard a concert in which a dead man sang with three friends on worldwide TV.

Ireland, to return to that most distressful country, has gone from a place "more Catholic than the pope" to legalized contraception in 1988 and legalized divorce in 1995.

Fewer and fewer American families can survive with one breadwinner. The marriage in which both partners work has become more and more common.

As the War Against Some Drugs escalates, usage of those drugs also increases. Somebody, somewhere, seriously misunderstands the situation.

Most of the gains achieved by labor unions in the last century have gotten lost in only 8 years, during the Reagan Era, and nobody seems very confident that the unions can stage a comeback.

Internet World for March 1996 says bluntly that "... regulatory and legislative policy cannot hope to keep pace with technological innovation. This legislative time-lag between what politicians understand and what is technologically operative today is an abyss.... The union of computers and telecommunications is primed to cause economic and political earthquakes." In other words, we more and more live with a technology that our alleged rulers do not understand well enough to regulate in any way.

Black helicopters hover above and some think they "only" mean to discover our forbidden farm-crops while others think they represent the first wave of UN or extraterrestrial conquest.

In an early work satirizing Republican paranoias, *Roosevelt After Inauguration*, William S. Burroughs has F.D.R. say "I'll force the motherfuckers to mutate!" I think that we can best understand our situation in terms of this sort of metaphor. I don't mean that Roosevelt did it, or that the UN did it, or that any fungible group acting alone did it. I think the laws of information have overloaded our circuits and we must mutate to survive. This neurological mutation has started, most of it taking weird and often absurd forms, but I don't think we can stop the process at this point.

As I have tried to prove in my nonfiction and dramatize in my fiction, *what we perceive depends on what we believe possible*, and as the latter changes, the former will change. Some new perceptions, like most new lifeforms, will not survive evolutionary testing; others will come to dominate the human world of the next century. What some have called my "blasphemous cheerfulness" (or my "cockeyed optimism") just depends on my basic agnosticism. We don't know the outcome of this worldwide transformation, so it seems sick and decadent (in the Nietzschean sense) when fashionable opinion harps on all the gloomy alternatives and resolutely ignores the utopian possibilities that seem, today, equally likely (and, on the basis of past evolution, perhaps a little more likely).

I regard it as late in the day to still cling to Christian and/or post-Christian masochism. Let us have the courage to think in less neurotic categories. The stars, now, look like they await us.

Robert Anton Wilson
Freedom, California
January 18, 1997

How to Read a Film Script

Scripts come in various forms, and usually get changed in the course of filming. I wrote this script as a director's final version, because, frankly I wanted to direct it as well as write it. (Well, we all have our delusions....) In other words, this script attempts to tell, in Hollywood format, just what the audience would see and hear in the finished version.

I used the terms and abbreviations known to everybody in the film business, but since most readers do not belong to that rather specialized group and since I remain filled with ardent desire to avoid all obscurity and make things as easy as possible for the common folks in Biloxi (for whom I, of course, intend all my books) I will define those terms here, as ready reference for any persons who find themselves a bit perplexed now and then.

To begin, a scene can take place indoors or outdoors. The abbreviation, INT. simply means INTERIOR, and tells the camera crew where to set up operations—on a sound-stage, not outdoors in a jungle, a desert, on a highway, etc. Similarly, EXT. means

EXTERIOR and tells us the camera people will get out and get some air and exercise.

Next, suppose a camera set-up stands in one place during a shot. Let us say the camera set-up stands at a considerable distance: we then have what we call a LONG SHOT. Move the set-up closer and we obviously have a MEDIUM SHOT. And, of course, move even closer and we have a CLOSE UP. Not too hard, right?

While the set-up stands in one place, the camera itself may move; we then have what the industry calls a PAN. You see that every time an actor talks and some-body else enters the scene: the camera PANS, just as your eyes would, to see who has entered. While the set-up remains stationary in this fashion, the camera may DOLLY IN for a CLOSE-UP.

The whole camera set-up may move. We then have a TRACKING SHOT, and you see that every time actors on horses or in cars chase other actors on horses or in cars.

The opening shot, for instance, says EXTERIOR: NIGHT—LONG TRACKING SHOT. The first phrase, EXTERIOR: NIGHT, means, as you might guess, that the events take place outdoors and at night (or that the lighting and set make it look like an outdoor night-time shot).[1] LONG TRACKING SHOT means that the camera will show a long view, rather than a medium or close view, and that the camera will move some dis-

---

[1] This happens when the whole "set" consists of a model on a table-top. The openings of, e.g., Orson Welles' *Citizen Kane* and Tim Burton's *Ed Wood* both look like outdoor tracking shots, but actually the camera only tracked and panned around table-top models in both cases.

tance. Since this shot shows the skyline of Boston, the cameraman would probably work from a helicopter.

Not too hard to understand so far, right?

Now later we will read of PANNING SHOTS, which differ from TRACKING SHOTS in that in a tracking shot the camera literally "tracks" the persons or objects we wish the audience to look at. Most pursuits in Westerns or cop movies, on horses or in cars, use TRACKING SHOTS; the most famous openings using such a tracking or pursuit structure appear in Welles's *Touch of Evil* and Altman's *The Player*. In a PANNING SHOT, the camera set-up does not move—it does not ride around on a crane or in a helicopter: it stays in one place. It turns, however, just the way you turn your head when conversing with several people at a party or in a crowd. A typical pan, indeed, usually occurs when some actor, playing a character who doesn't know what's coming down, might look from one speaker to another trying to read their faces for clues: the camera pans instead of the actor and we see what he/she would see.

The abbreviation, V.O. means VOICE OVER. In that case we hear an actor/actress without seeing them. Perhaps the most common use of V.O. occurs when the director wants to show an actor responding to another actor's words. VOICE OVER also occurs frequently as we enter a flashback to an earlier time: the actor/actress says something like, "It started last Christmas. I remember decorating the tree..." The first line will usually occur normally: you see the speaker speaking the words you hear. The second line occurs in V.O. as you see the scene on Christmas day with the tree and its decorations.

V.O. not only gives the camera more flexibility and "eloquence," but also, of course, allows for the correction of errors. Sharp viewers will sometimes catch this, noticing that the actor's mouth movements do not match the words heard. In this case, the actor got part of the line wrong, but the director liked the scene enough to save it, and actor just did the line again somewhere else, whereupon the Sound Mixer added it in the right place.

Transitions from one shot to another usually take the form of a CUT. You see one scene and then abruptly to you see another. If it happened in ordinary space, you would fear for your sanity, or suspect that somebody slipped you a Mickey, but in film we all accept these quantum jumps quite casually.

Occasionally, in place of a CUT we may have a FADE. We do not jump: the scene just dies away and we become conscious of a blank space before the next scene begins. This functions like the end of a chapter in a novel, or the curtain falling to end a scene or an act on the stage.

P.O.V. means "point of view" and serves the same function as the novelist's "From where I sat I saw a Rolls-Royce pull up across the street and an expensively-dressed blonde got out—with a pair of legs worth looking at twice or even three times." (Well, a novelist of the Chandler school might write it that way.) In film, the camera's P.O.V. shows what the novel only describes: we see the car pull up, the blonde get out and a close-up of the legs worth looking at, all from the narrator's point of view. You see P.O.V. in most movies, once or twice; Hitchcock used it extensively in the early parts of *Psycho* where a large percentage of shots show

Marion Crane's point of view, thus building up audience identification with her and adding immensely to the shock effect of the shower scene. The only film ever projected with every shot seen from the narrator's P.O.V. and he never appearing on screen (for the same reason you never see yourself) was Orson Welles' *Heart of Darkness*, written but never filmed, alas. Robert Montgomery's *Lady in the Lake* used the narrator's P.O.V. in most shots, but he appeared onscreen between segments to explain why he did whatever he did in the last scene, an awkward dilution of the Welles innovation.

I have never shared the popular view that screenplays make harder reading than novels, and I hope that with these brief explanations you will find this script no more murky than *Finnegans Wake* or *Gravity's Rainbow*.

The Walls Came Tumbling Down

Un Film de Robert Anton Wilson

EXTERIOR: NIGHT—LONG TRACKING SHOT

The skyline of Boston and Cambridge. Weird electronic music.

EXTERIOR: NIGHT—MEDIUM SHOT

A car is racing down an empty suburban street in Cambridge.

EXTERIOR: NIGHT—MEDIUM CLOSE SHOT

Through the window of the car we see MICHAEL ELLIS, a bearded, professorial, middle-aged man obviously gripped by powerful anxiety.

EXTERIOR: NIGHT—CAMBRIDGE STREET, TRACKING SHOT

The car shrieks to a halt. Music is faster, more ominous. MICHAEL gets out, forgets to lock the door, rushes across a lawn, approaches a tall, gabled New England house.

EXTERIOR: NIGHT—MEDIUM SHOT

MICHAEL is banging on the door of the house.

INTERIOR—SHOT FROM BOTTOM OF
STAIRCASE

*Darkness. Light comes on suddenly and we see
SIMON SELENE in his bathrobe and pajamas,
half asleep and irritable, at the top of the stairs. He
is also bearded and, right now, his hair is unruly.*

SIMON   All right, all right, all right—I'm
                     coming. (*To himself:*) And if it's not
                     a message from the Nobel Prize
                     Committee I'll shoot you.

EXTERIOR LONG SHOT—THE STREET

*Another car pulls up behind Michael's. Camera
pans in toward car window. We see a tough but
well-dressed man, who may well be some kind of
cop or federal agent.*

MAN   Subject has entered a house on Lois
(*into   Lane. Address is two niner niner
microphone on   three.
dash*)

INTERIOR—SIMON'S KITCHEN. MEDIUM
SHOT.

*Simon is making coffee. Michael sits in a chair,
barely able to control his abnormal state of agita-
tion and elation.*

MICHAEL You're a psychologist. You have to
tell me whether I'm crazy or not. If
I'm not crazy, this is the greatest scientific breakthrough of our age.

SIMON You don't seem crazy, Mike. In my
(*supportive,* opinion you are merely suffering
friendly) from some sort of traumatic shock.
I've seen men look worse just from
being audited by IRS.

He places the two cups of coffee on the table.

SIMON Why don't you just tell me about it
(*fully awake,* from the very beginning?
professional,
"objective")

NEW ANGLE—CLOSE UP ON MICHAEL

MICHAEL Christ, it's been going on for years.
All my life maybe. But well … the
fear started last year. You were
there that night, with Tree. You
remember—I was being very
obnoxious.…

Fade to:

INTERIOR—TIGHT CLOSE-UP

A key is being held in a man's hand. Weird music.

MICHAEL It started with that phoney psy-
(*V.O.*) chic—Stokowski or whatever his
name was …

As we watch, the key is starting to curl upwards very slowly.

SIMON (V.O.)   Katzinski, I think ...

The key has now curled upward into a beautifully smooth parabolic curve.

TV HOST (V.O.)   Was this key bent by the power of the mind—psychic power—as Mr. Kowalski claims? Or is Mr. Kowalski just a clever magician, as skeptics charge?

MICHAEL   Oh, bullshit, bullshit, bullshit! If
ELLIS (V.O.)   he's not a fake, I'll moon the Archbishop on Saint Patrick's Day!

INTERIOR—SLOW PANNING SHOT: ELLIS
LIVING ROOM

The camera on the TV show pans back to show HOST holding key, and Mr. Kowalski, a balding, ordinary man, trying his best to look smug and inscrutable. Our camera also pans back to reveal the living room of Michael and Cathy Ellis.

The standard of living is upper middle class, but somewhat untidy: there are lots and lots of lots of books. Michael and Cathy are both Professors. Both are in their 50s but "well preserved." He has slightly greying beard and looks like the kind of scientist who keeps up with the football scores; she has one streak of grey in her fiery red hair, and is "sensibly" dressed. Impressionist paintings on the walls express Cathy's taste; a single Star Trek *poster reveals something still boyish in Michael.*

Mike punches the remote control and Johnny Carson appears on the TV. We do not hear him, because Mike and Cathy talk over him.

In a third seat, off in a corner, is Prof. Simon Selene; we can now see that he is about 10 years younger than Mike and Cathy; he is also abnormally watchful and observant.

Beside SIMON sits TREE, a female graduate student, disturbingly sexy. Her legs are crossed and well worth looking at, as Chandler would say.

CATHY *(assertive, the Liberated lady)*	Damn it, Mike, I wanted to see more of that.
MICHAEL	Why? To fill your mind with garbage? Any stage magician could do that trick.

NEW ANGLE—SIMON IN FOREGROUND

Simon is amused at the bickering as it proceeds.

CATHY	I can decide for myself what's garbage, thank you. I'm a great big girl now. Mommy lets me blow my own nose and go to the bathroom all alone and everything.
MICHAEL *(reasonable tone)*	Cathy, darling, you're a scientist.

CATHY   Does that mean I should be a bigot?
                               I thought it meant the opposite.

MICHAEL   Jesus ... women! The feminine
(*flaring up*)   mind! God's second mistake!

CATHY   Jesus ... men! The masculine mind!
(*striding over to*   God's first mistake!
speak right in his
face)

MICHAEL   Let's not start the Sex War again.
                               You know that Wackalski guy is a
                               fake. Why are you trying to annoy
                               me?

NEW ANGLE—TREE IN FOREGROUND

Her long miniskirted legs dominate the shot.

CATHY   I wish just once in my life I could be
                               as sure of anything as you are of
                               everything!

MICHAEL   Are you a mathematical physicist or
                               a gypsy card reader?

CATHY   Are you a mathematical physicist or
                               the Pope of Rome?

Pause while they glare at each other.

JOHNNY   It got so boring that we finally went
CARSON   to a motel and yelled "Vice Squad!"
(*from the TV*)   and then ran around the back to
                               watch the Evangelists climbing out
                               the windows in their drawers.

Simon finds this hilarious and cracks up. Michael and Cathy start to laugh, too, and the tension is temporarily broken.

MICHAEL

Oh, what the hell—that psychic stuff is kind of funny.... The only thing that isn't funny is that some people take it seriously. That's what scares me.

TREE
(*in a nasal, unsexy voice*)

Yeah, you guys. Kiss and make up. Quarrels make bad karma.

Michael hands the remote to Cathy, bowing courteously..

CATHY
(*humorous, pretending formality*)

Thank you, Dr. Ellis.

MICHAEL
(*also pretending stiffness*)

You are welcome, Dr. Ellis.

They kiss. TREE simpers with delight. Cathy punches the remote.

INTERIOR—CLOSE UP. DR. GENE SCOTT

TV's most egregious evangelist is in rare form, wearing a funny hat, puffing a cigar, and orating earnestly.

DR. SCOTT

... all the way through the Bible, from Genesis to Revelations. You

can read every sentence, and you
won't find the word "audit" even
once. That's not part of the word of
God.

CATHY (*V.O.*)   Damn it, this thing isn't working.

MICHAEL   Here, honey, give it to me.
(*V.O.*)

DR. SCOTT   And another proof that IRS is the
                   Beast 666 ...

*Click. Blurry lines. We are on the original channel
again.*

INTERIOR—MEDIUM SHOT. TV STUDIO

*The HOST is now sitting in an easy chair facing a
Dumpy Little Housewife in an identical easy chair.*

HOST   And how long have you been chan-
                   neling ah Mr. Gonad?

INTERIOR—THE ELLIS LIVING ROOM

*Michael and Cathy are back in their seats. Michael
nervously lights a cigarette. We can see the TV
more or less as they do.*

HOUSEWIFE   He doesn't call himself Mr. Gonad.
                   Just Gonad. Sometimes he calls
                   himself Gonad the Barbarian. I
                   think it's a title of some sort. You
                   must remember he lived 100,000
                   years ago.

Simon is amused again and smothers a laugh.

SIMON   *Gonad the Barbarian!*

HOST   Um yes. And how long have you
                         been channeling him?

CATHY   This is the sort of thing the majority
(*to Simon, but   of Americans believe, Simon. We
obviously   should try to understand instead of
speaking also for   just standing by and feeling supe-
Michael's ears*)   rior.

MICHAEL   That's right. And if they take it into
(*mock serious*)   their moronic heads to start burn-
                         ing witches or Jews again, we
                         should try to keep an open mind
                         and—

TREE   Hey, Professor Ellis, just because we
                         got different ideas than you doesn't
                         mean we're Nazis....

SIMON   Mike, cool it, will you? Listen to
                         the show and editorialize later.

INTERIOR—MEDIUM SHOT: THE TV STUDIO

The HOST and Housewife are still talking.

HOST   And could you channel ah Gonad
                         right now for our audience?

MICHAEL   I'll be as quiet as a mouse. Or a
(*V.O.*)   Good German.

CATHY
(V.O.—low, intense)

Jesus, Mike!

NEW ANGLE—THE LIVING ROOM

TREE
(aloof, lofty)

All highly evolved beings remember their past lives.

SIMON

Tree, don't make it worse.

MICHAEL
(suddenly on a new tangent)

Is your name really "Tree," young lady?

TREE
(defensively)

Yes, and I've got a sister named Leaf and a brother named Bud.

MICHAEL

Your parents were at Woodstock, I presume.

TREE

Woodstock, the Pentagon demonstration ... the whole 60s scene....

MICHAEL
(deciding to be urbane)

Tree, Leaf and Bud. Are you going to name your first child Seed?

Their voices have drowned out the Housewife, but we see that she is starting to go into a trance.

INTERIOR—TV STUDIO. CLOSE UP

The housewife's face sinks down toward sleep, then a new expression appears slowly. She opens her eyes again and begins to speak in a totally unconvincing imitation of a male voice.

HOUSEWIFE   I, Gonad, greet you over the magic
                   picture box, people of what you call
                   the 20th Century.

MICHAEL   She's not talking to the Moslems, I
(*V.O.*)   guess. It's the 13th Century to them.
                   And for the Jews it's ...

SIMON (*V.O.*)   For pity's sake, Mike ... and for all
                   our sakes ...

HOUSEWIFE   I have returned to tell you that all is
                   one. The black man and the white
                   man are brothers. The woman is the
                   soul or as you would say the mag-
                   netic pole of the male. Limit noth-
                   ing. Those whom you call
                   extraterrestrials are your inner souls
                   ...

INTERIOR—MEDIUM SHOT: THE ELLIS LIVING
ROOM

*Simon in foreground, TREE and CATHY on oppo-
site side of TV.*

TREE   Wow, this is real heavy. Sex is like a
                   magnetic pole.

NEW ANGLE—MICHAEL IN FOREGROUND

*He is obviously looking at TREE's legs and enjoy-
ing them, as much as Mr. Chandler's Mr. Marlowe
would.*

CLOSE-UP—CATHY

She observes the direction of Michael's gaze and looks unhappy. She is obviously thinking that she is over 50 and TREE is only around 22.

MEDIUM SHOT—MICHAEL AND CATHY

MICHAEL observes that CATHY has caught him in a voyeuristic fantasy and coughs on his cigarette smoke.

MICHAEL	How can he be dead 100,000 years
(*loudly*)	and still be such a thundering bore?
	Jesus—sex and magnetism. That
	was every guy's make-out line when
	I was young, back in the 50s ...

CLOSE-UP—TREE

TREE	You don't understand. It's like the
(*nasal, sincere*)	*yin* and *yang* in China ...

MICHAEL	Or is it the Poon and the Tang in
(*V.O.*)	Okinawa? Or the Hodge and the
	Podge in Los Angeles?

TREE registers hurt. Simon leans over to pat her hand and starts to speak. We see Michael moving rapidly and hear a door slam. The camera pans back to make clear that Michael has stomped out of the room in a huff. Cathy makes a humorous gesture of resignation to Tree.

SIMON	It's okay, Cathy. All creative people
	get these ... moods.

CATHY   Is that your opinion as a psychologist?

SIMON   It's my opinion as a friend.

CATHY   He gets more of these ... moods ...
(*serious and*   as he gets older.
worried)

TREE   He probably eats too much red meat. Vegetarians don't get so moody. Or else it's coffee. You should serve him Decaf.

HOUSEWIFE   You contain infinite space and the
(*from TV*)   infinite stars thereof. At the bottom of Hell are the stairs of Paradise.

Eerie music. Cut to:

INTERIOR—MEDIUM CLOSE. THE ELLIS
BEDROOM

Camera tilted at 45° angle and eerie music continues. Michael is pacing the floor, furious. He lights another cigarette. Then he stops walking and stares at this hand, surprised to see that it is trembling. Camera moves in to Michael's face as he watches his hand tremble. His eyes show only clinical scientific detachment as he observes the tremor of his own emotion.

MICHAEL   I knew I was having an anxiety
(*V.O.*)   attack—all the classic Freudian symptoms, heart pounding, loss of breath, dizziness—but I didn't

know why. I could have shit a barrel of bricks ... and I didn't... know
... why ...

SIMON
(*V.O.—softly*)

You were attracted to a woman
much younger than yourself ...

MICHAEL
(*V.O.*)

Yes, but.... I was starting to remember something I'd forgotten ... and
it frightened me ...

EXTERIOR—A HILL IN JERUSALEM (FLASH CUT)

*This shot is so brief the audience cannot quite take
it all in. Michael in Roman officer's uniform, 30
years younger and beardless, rams his sword into a
crucified man. Blood spurts onto Michael's uniform. Quick cut:*

EXTERIOR—CAMBRIDGE/BOSTON SKYLINE

MICHAEL
(*V.O.*)

It stayed with me.... I felt that I was
about to pick up a corner of the
universe and see what was down
there, under the carpet ...

EXTERIOR—STREET IN CAMBRIDGE. TRACKING SHOT

*Light music. Michael is walking toward M.I.T.,
briefcase in hand. He passes a newsstand and camera zooms in to highlight a headline on a sleazo
tabloid:*

BABY BORN WITH
EGYPTIAN BRACELET
Stunning Proof of Reincarnation

Music hits sour chord as Camera pans to Michael looking angry and disgusted.

MICHAEL   It was like being in Nazi Germany
(*V.O.*)   ... knowing what was coming ...

EXTERIOR—ANOTHER STREET IN
CAMBRIDGE. TRACKING SHOT

Christmas music. Michael and Cathy come out of a store, loaded with packages. Camera zooms to highlight another tabloid headline:

WORLD WAR II BOMBER
FOUND ON THE MOON!
SCIENTISTS BAFFLED!

Music hits sour chord as Camera pans to Michael looking angry and disgusted.

EXTERIOR—ANOTHER STREET IN
CAMBRIDGE. TRACKING SHOT

Rock music. Michael and Simon come out of the bar we shall see often later in the film. Both are a bit drunk and quite mellow. Camera zooms to highlight a third tabloid haiku:

Woman's Tale of Terror:
"I WAS RAPED BY MIDGETS FROM MARS!"

Music turns sour as Camera pans to Michael looking angry and disgusted.

MICHAEL   I was traveling back in time.... The
(V.O.)   Dark Ages were being reborn all
                     around me....

EXTERIOR—ANOTHER STREET IN
CAMBRIDGE. TRACKING SHOT

*Michael comes out of barber shop and sees another
tabloid headline.*

**MAD HUNCHBACK SELLS HUNCH TO BUTCHER:
WOMAN POISONED BY HUNCHBURGER**

*Sour music as we close on headline; we don't even
see Michael's reaction this time.*

INTERIOR—A LARGE AUDITORIUM,
HARVARD. TRACKING SHOT

*The room is full of cameras and other media equip-
ment. Scientists (all white, male and middle-aged)
sit at a table in front. They wear armbands saying
SSA, with the SS's represented by lightning bolts. A
banner above the table explains the initials, saying
SCIENTIFIC   SKEPTICS   ASSOCIATION.
Michael is at the podium reading a press release.
Musical theme:*

Beethoven's "Ode to Joy."

As music fades we begin to hear Michael's speech.

MICHAEL   ... and all the superstitions of the
                     Dark Ages seem to have returned.
                     Astrology, the most absurd of all
                     pseudo-sciences. Reincarnation,

the last hope of losers everywhere. The crazy UFO mystique, our modern form of the primitive cargo cults. In this atmosphere some of us in the scientific community have decided it is necessary to remind the world of the lessons it should have learned in the 18th Century. The value of reason, of caution, of skepticism...

Pan to:

LONG SHOT—BACK OF AUDIENCE

Newspaper Reporter and TV cameraman are in foreground.

REPORTER   Who's that guy at the podium now?

CAMERAMAN   Dr. Ellis. Big man in the physics department at Harvard. Works for the government and M.I.T., too.

MICHAEL   The Scientific Skeptics Association
(*V.O.*)   will be a policeman seeking out fraud and deception in the so-called New Age cults that are mostly fronts for a revival of the superstitions of the Dark Ages ...

His voice bridges over to the beginning of the next scene.

INTERIOR—A BAR IN CAMBRIDGE

The walls are covered with computer-generated fractals (which look like modern art to those who do not recognize them).

MICHAEL comes out of the men's room and encounters TREE, again dressed in a sexy outfit and carrying books on Tarot and astrology.

MICHAEL   Ah, good evening, Miss Forest.

TREE   Tree. Its not Forest. Its just Tree.

MICHAEL   Don't tell anybody. My rivals on the
(*twinkling*)   faculty will all be saying I can't tell
                 the Forests from the Trees.

TREE (*direct and*   Wanna buy me a beer?
to the point)

MICHAEL   Ah, I ... ah....

Camera pans slowly down over Tree's curvy young body. Fade to:

EXTERIOR—MEDIUM TRACKING SHOT

We are in the front seat of a coupé with the top down. Michael is driving. He and Tree are both hilarious. The car is speeding.

MICHAEL   It's the first time I smoked it since
(*happy as a clam*) the '60s.

TREE (*giggling*)   I thought you were the type who
                 never smoked it.

MICHAEL   In the 60s we had to. Otherwise the
                 students would think we were a
                 bunch of old farts.

TREE   You—an old fart?

This sends them both into new gales of laughter.
Cut to:

TIGHT CLOSE UP: MICHAEL AND TREE

Both are gasping rhythmically, although there is an
astrological calendar behind her and it is obvious
that they are standing up.

TREE   Ah.... ahahah Jesus, Jesus....

Camera pans back enough to reveal that they are
having intercourse on a study table crammed with
books. She still has most of her clothes on;
Michael's trousers are around his ankles. Cut to:

LONG SHOT: TREE'S ROOM

Punk Rock is blaring from a stereo. Way in the
back of the room, on a futon on the floor, Michael
and Tree are having intercourse again. Cut to:

CLOSE-UP: MICHAEL'S FACE

He is obviously about to have an orgasm again.
Camera pans down and we see he is sitting naked
on the futon. We glimpse Tree's head bobbing up
and down above his crotch. The Punk Rock blares
to a climax.

TREE'S ROOM—LONG TRACKING SHOT

We hear Tree's voice before the camera finds her, sitting on the futon, a cover partly wrapped around her against the cold. Michael is lying down, finishing a marijuana cigarette.

TREE (*very softly, less nasal, intense*)

... so I did the cards again. And Death came up again. I was getting freaked. I shuffled them five or six times and cut them over and over and shuffled some more ... and Death came up the third time. I just packed everything and moved out of there. Stayed with Leaf in Berkeley for a while. Then I heard about the fire—everybody in the building was killed. All my friends in Ann Arbor. I would have been barbecued myself if I had stayed there. You can have your scientific skepticism, professor. That was one case where my superstitions kept me alive.

She turns, looks down at him.

TREE

Well, aren't you going to tell me it was just a coincidence?

MICHAEL

No, not now. Not while you're reliving the grief.

She curls up in his arms. He holds her affection-
ately. Camera pans in slowly and we see a strange,
wondering look in his eyes. Fade to:

INTERIOR—A PIZZERIA IN CAMBRIDGE

The walls are covered with John Lennon and
James Dean posters. The juke box is playing Sid
Vicious & The Sex Pistols. A large sign says, TRY
OUR ORGANIC VEGETARIAN PIZZA.

Michael enters with Simon Selene. They wait to be
served, continuing an argument.

SIMON	Mike, okay, okay—I'm not an ordained and anointed physicist like you. I'm just a lowly clinical psychologist. I admit it. But damn it all—
MICHAEL (*agitated, but with a mask of calm*)	Simon, Simon. Just listen a minute.
SIMON	But I had to study as much statistics as you did to get my degree. I did the study in good faith, using accepted statistical techniques. And you're asking me to bury it? Hide it?

A waitress approaches.

WAITRESS (*picking Simon to address*)	Will it be smoking or non-smoking, sir?
SIMON (*absently*)	Non-smoking.
MICHAEL (*poker-faced, firm*)	Smoking, white Protestant.
WAITRESS (*jarred*)	Beg your pardon, sir?
MICHAEL (*still poker-faced*)	Smoking, white Protestant.
WAITRESS (*out of her depth*)	I can't do that, sir. It's illegal.
MICHAEL (*icy cold*)	If we must have segregation, I want my own form of segregation. Smoking, white Protestant. Filter tips only. No Chicanos within ten tables even if they're Seventh Day Adventists or Jehovah's Witnesses.
SIMON (*easily*)	Mike, cut it out. I'm the one you're furious at, not her.
MICHAEL (*his voice cracking*)	I am not furious, Dr. Selene. I am merely trying to make you see reason.
SIMON (*to Waitress*)	Smoking, please.

INTERIOR—A TABLE IN THE PIZZERIA

Simon and Mike have beers. Mike is smoking. On the wall behind them is another poster showing two scientists examing computer print-out graphs; one of them is saying "Anybody who thinks he understands the data is full of shit."

SIMON You and your colleagues on the SSA hired me to do a study. I did the study. It didn't suit your prejudices. And—

MICHAEL It's not a question of prejudice, Simon. It's a question of not stepping into an open gopher hole ...

SIMON Bullshit. Gauquelin found that some astrological predictions are accurate with Europeans he selected at random. The SSA hired me to do an objective study of comparative data. I did an objective study and I found that the same astrological predictions are accurate for randomly selected Americans. You want me to bury my study. If that isn't prejudice, what the hell would you call it?

MICHAEL Damn it, Simon, nobody said you should bury the data. But your results are unreasonable and inexplicable. We just want you to postpone publication until further studies can be done. That isn't prejudice. It's normal scientific caution.

SIMON	When somebody says statistical results are unreasonable that means his prejudices are offended. Period.
MICHAEL	Damn it, you sound like you believe in astrology.
SIMON	Which I do not. You aren't listening to me. What is at stake here is not whether some one part of astrology is true or false, but whether we accept data as it comes or bury the data we don't understand.
MICHAEL	But ... but ...
SIMON (*less heated, more the therapist*)	Mike, seriously, you ought to ask yourself what it is that you're really afraid of. You weren't angry at the waitress but at me. And you're not afraid of this minor statistical correlation but of something it symbolizes.

Camera tilts slightly and moves in toward close up on Michael.

MICHAEL (*forced laugh*)	I didn't come to you to be psychoanalyzed, Dr. Selene. Besides, I thought your whole profession abandoned Freud for chemicals twenty years ago.

NEW ANGLE—SIMON AND MICHAEL,
MEDIUM CLOSE

SIMON

Each of us has an iron barrier we're afraid to lift.... You'll have to face it someday, Mike. What is it you fear so much?

MICHAEL
(*mask off,
furious*)

Oh, stop this Voodoo hocus-pocus. I've had enough.

He rises to leave, and suddenly freezes, contorted by pain.

SIMON
(*suddenly
showing his
friendship*)

Mike, Mike, what's the matter?

Michael sinks back into his chair.

MICHAEL (*in
agony*)

A tooth-ache ... Christ! I never knew it could be this bad ... must be abcessing. Jesus, oh, Jesus ...

SIMON

Is Dr. Riley still your dentist?

MICHAEL
(*barely able to
speak*)

Yes.

SIMON

I'll call him and tell him it's an emergency. Meanwhile, take one of these.

He hands a prescription bottle across the table.

MICHAEL

What is it?

SIMON	Pain-killer. A Codeine analog. It'll make you drowsy, but don't worry. I'll drive you to Riley's office. I'll call Cathy to pick you up—I've got a class in an hour.
MICHAEL *(weak grin)*	Thank you for not saying this is psychosomatic.
SIMON *(not grinning, worried)*	You can deal with that later. Right now, the important thing is to stop your pain.

Simon exits to front of Pizzeria.

INTERIOR—CLOSE UP: VIEW FROM BELOW

Michael's hands dominate the shot. He has the prescription bottle in his right hand, facing camera, struggling desperately with the top.

| MICHAEL (V.O.) | Another goddam adult-proof top. They call them child-proof. What nonsense. There isn't a child in the world without the curiosity and patience to get into one of these. It's the adults who give up and say, "Ah, shit, I don't need the pills that much." Well, I do need them. I'll get it open if I have to smash it on the table. |

The top comes off the bottle suddenly and pills scatter in all directions. Michael shows fury as pills spatter screen and we fade to:

INTERIOR—MEDIUM CLOSE SUBJECTIVE SHOT

Camera is in the position of Michael Ellis in a dentist's chair. We see what he sees. a corner of wall and ceiling and the face of Dr. Riley, the dentist, in mid-frame. The dentist extends toward the camera (Michael) a fiendish-looking, somewhat surrealistic instrument never seen in a dental clinic on Earth.

DR. RILEY   Open wider, please.

The instrument comes closer and we blur to fadeout.

INTERIOR—SUBJECTIVE SHOT, MOVING CAR

Camera is in position of Michael Ellis in front seat, next to Cathy. We see normal scenes of downtown Cambridge, then a very brief oddity—a train appears in the street, doors open, and a Honor Guard unloads a coffin draped in an American flag.

CATHY (V.O.)   How are we doing, lover?

Camera turns in seat to look at Cathy.

MICHAEL   I think I'm hallucinating. In fact, I
(V.O.)   *know* I'm hallucinating.

Bird shadows fall across front of car. Ominous music.

CATHY (*brisk,*   That's just the sodium pentothol.
no-nonsense)   Dr. Riley warned you about it,

remember? 81 per cent of all subjects ...

MICHAEL   ... experience hallucinations or leth-
(V.O.)   argy. I remember. And I've also got
                 some damned analog of Codeine in
                 me.

*The music speeds up as a small light in front of the
car expands to a giant rainbow spinning-wheel
that flickers on/off rapidly, briefly resembles a
UFO, then covers the screen as we cut to:*

INTERIOR—SUBJECTIVE SHOT, THE ELLIS
LIVING ROOM

*Camera is in position of Michael on couch, looking
around warily then relaxing and looking up at ceiling. Cathy appears leaning over him.*

CATHY   Comfy, Michael?

MICHAEL   I'm okay. No pain yet.
(V.O., *mumbling*
drowsily)

CATHY   I'll put on some Bach. If you must
                 hallucinate, you might as well hal-
                 lucinate pretty things. Right?

*Angry face of giant buzzard comes between Cathy
and camera as music holds one shrieking note.*

MICHAEL   Uh ... right ...
(V.O.—
uncertainly)

Cathy moves off camera. Sound of stereo being opened and compact disc inserted. The first bars of Bach's "Toccata and Fugue."

CATHY (V.O.) Just call me if you need anything.

Sound of Cathy walking to another room. Bach continues. The camera remains fixed on the corner of the ceiling for 10 seconds (which seems longer to the audience, waiting for something to happen).

MICHAEL Uh, Cathy.... (*Pause.*) ... Didn't
(V.O.) hear me. Oh, well, I'm okay. I am really okay. I know I'm okay ...

INTERIOR—OBJECTIVE SHOT FROM CEILING

We are looking directly down at the room and see Michael on the couch. His eyes are closed and his mouth does not move as he speaks again.

MICHAEL See myself as others see me.... This,
(V.O.—*elated* gentlemen, is called an out-of-body
yet agitated) experience. Just a hallucination, of course. We are trained scientists here and will not be deluded by a drug reaction. Right? Right! Absolutely. (*Pause.*) I hope.

EXTERIOR—OBJECTIVE SHOT FROM SKY

We are looking down at Mike and Cathy's house from above. We see the house, the lawn with hedges and driveway.

MICHAEL   Jesus Christ on a crutch! (*Pause.*)
(*V.O.*)   Just a hallucination. Remember
        that. A drug reaction. Codeine and
        sodium pentothol. You are not
        really out of your body, Dr. Ellis....
        I think right now we must say,
        speaking scientifically, that you're
        just a few bricks shy of a full load
        ... scientifically, that is, you don't
        have all your dogs on the same
        leash ... (*slight moan of fear*)

INTERIOR, THE LIVING ROOM—NEW ANGLE

We see Michael on the couch. He half sits up and looks around.

MICHAEL   There. I'm still in my body. (*Pause.*)
(*V.O.*)   But I wasn't in my body when I
        looked down at the house from
        above....

INSERT

An abstract flesh-colored blur with dark shadows. Cut to:

MEDIUM SHOT—SLOW MOTION

The Honor Guard unloading the flag-draped coffin from the train. The sound of a bugle playing "Taps."

INSERT

The flesh-colored shadowy blur. Camera pans back and we see it is a human hand with a nail being driven through it. Cut to:

INTERIOR, THE LIVING ROOM—NEW ANGLE

Michael sits full upright on the couch, suddenly terrified.

SIMON (V.O.)   Each of us has an iron curtain we're afraid to lift ... no, an iron barrier ...

EXTERIOR TRACKING SHOT: SANTA CRUZ, CAL.

Camera pans across Santa Cruz hills at dizzy speed (using zoom lens to accelerate pan). We move in on a comfortable ranch house and hear a phone ringing. Suspense music.

MICHAEL (V.O.)   The house where I was born. Look Romeward, angel. No, look homeward.

INTERIOR: FRONT HALL OF THE RANCH HOUSE

Camera pans down hall to move into close-up on the phone, then pans back to reveal a boy— Michael Ellis, age 12—picking up the phone. He holds it to his ear and we move in to tighter close up on the phone and ear. We hear a melodious, solemn, somewhat angelic voice speak to the boy. Soft suspense music.

| MYSTERY VOICE | Hello again, Michael. This is your friend above. You are doing well at school and we are pleased but you must concentrate more— |

| MICHAEL (*with childish directness*) | Are you *really* an angel? Can you *fly*? |

| MYSTERY VOICE (*not registering question*) | ... you must concentrate more on physics and mathematics. Remember that you are our chosen one. Remember that you are our creation just as we are ... |

A hand appears on screen, grabbing the phone from Michael. Camera pans back and up as we hear:

| MYSTERY VOICE | ... your creation. Remember that we have selected only you ... |

Camera has panned back to reveal Michael's mother, Laura, a harassed and very angry woman of about 45.

| LAURA (*into phone*) | Listen, you nut, you better stop this, I'm warning you. I'll go to the police, I will, you crazy son of a bitch. Playing jokes like this on a harmless little boy, you should have your head examined, mister. |

Camera pans back to reveal Michael frightened and confused and, behind him on the wall, the calendar with the date: AUGUST 6, 1945.

MICHAEL   I didn't know what to think ...
(V.O.)

Quick cut to:

INTERIOR: STUDENT BEDROOM

Poster of very young Elvis on the wall. Michael Ellis, beardless, 30 years younger than the mature man who is remembering this, is in bed with Cathy, also 30 years younger. The bed is mussed, indicating recent dalliance. Mike is smoking a cigarette and Cathy is munching pizza.

MICHAEL   I mean, I trusted my mother, but the
(*continuing*)   guy on the phone was a really
                world-class put-on artist. He had
                me going, I tell you.

CATHY (*slight   It is a creepy kind of joke, Mike.
Southern accent*) How many of those calls did you
                get all together?

MICHAEL   I don't know anymore. Six or seven
                maybe. All around Hiroshima Day.

CATHY   But he stopped after your mother
(*munching*)   chewed him out?

MICHAEL (*a bit Totally. Not another word out of
sorry?*)   him.

CATHY   I'll bet you more than half believed
(*teasing*)   him. That's why you're here at Cal
                Tech majoring in physics. Like he
                told you to. You'd still like to

believe him, wouldn't you? Have an angel on your team at exam time?

MICHAEL
(*teasing back*)

Well, wouldn't you want to be the Chosen One of Heaven? The Elect. The Servant of the Lord.

CATHY

That's Joe McCarthy, according to my father. There can't be two Chosen Ones. Joe was sent to save us from the Godless Reds or is it from Tooth Decay? I forget.

NEW ANGLE

Close up on Michael and Cathy. He puts out his cigarette and begins to caress her again and kiss her neck erotically.

MICHAEL
(*with mock patience*)

When the Lord saw that we were threatened with Godless Reds, He sent Senator Joe. When He saw that were were threatened with Tooth Decay, he sent New Crest. With Frammis Steroid. Or is that Stannous Fluoride?

CATHY
(*becoming aroused but hiding it*)

Well, anyway, if you were a real American from Tennessee, like me, you would have had more to worry about.

MICHAEL (*also aroused*)

More than Tooth Decay or Senator Joe?

CATHY   Oh, yes, more ... and worse ... any
(*responding more*   good Baptist would tell you ...
visibly)

Camera pans in to close up on Cathy's lips.

MICHAEL   Tell me what?
(*V.O.*)

CATHY (*panting*   That creatures who claim to be
a bit)   angels may be devils ... demons
                         from hell—trying enter you and ...

The camera remains tight on her lips, swelling with
eroticism.

MICHAEL   Enter *me*? And?
(*V.O.*)

CATHY   Oh, darling, darling ...
(*control lost*)

MICHAEL   Cathy ... Cathy ... I love you ...
(*V.O.*)

Quick cut to:

SPECIAL EFFECT

The dentist, now a bald dwarf, extends the fiendish
instrument toward us.

MICHAEL   Cathy ... Cathy ... I love you ...
(*V.O.—without*
the intonation
and passion of
the first reading,
just
remembering)

Cut rapidly to:

REPEAT SHOT—TREE'S ROOM

Michael and Tree having sex standing/leaning on the study desk. Cut to:

LONG SHOT—THE STUDENT BEDROOM AT CAL TECH

The bed is jumping up and down, but not from the passion of Mike and Cathy. Everything in the room is jumping up and down. Cathy and Mike are both terrified. The general effect recalls The Exorcist *or* Poltergeist. *Cut to:*

INTERIOR—HOSPITAL ROOM

We see Cathy in childbirth, panting rhythmically. Cut to:

EXTERIOR LONG SHOT—BEACH

Michael and Cathy in bathing suits, running. A small child runs with them.

INTERIOR—THE CAL TECH BEDROOM: NEXT MORNING

Camera pans to find Cathy serving breakfast to Mike in a small alcove.

CATHY (*she still has a trace of Southern accent*)   That was quite a tremor last night. Felt like about five on the Richter.

MICHAEL
(*with eyes in
textbook on
physics*)

Um. What?

CATHY (*seating
herself*)

That was quite a quake last night, I
said.

MICHAEL
(*putting book
down*)

What? There was a quake last
night?

CATHY (*a bit
confused*)

Of course there was. Michael,
what's the matter? You weren't
asleep. We were — you know ...
making love.

MICHAEL
(*more distressed
than he should
be*)

What the hell are you talking
about? There was no quake while I
was awake.

CATHY (*voice
rising*)

But it couldn't have been a dream!

MICHAEL
(*lighting
cigarette,
nervous*)

It must have been a dream, Cathe-
rine Anne. I swear to God I don't
remember any earthquake.

CATHY
(*unreasonably
desperate*)

But Mike, honest, we were both
awake. We were ... making love ...

*The frame freezes on the two of them mouths
open, confused, frightened of something they cannot even think about. Cut to:*

EXTERIOR MEDIUM SHOT—THE BEACH: MIKE, CATHY AND CHILD

Thunder strikes. Michael is aghast. We pan in on the child, a boy, and the frame freezes as we hear the mournful sound of "Taps" being played.

Fade to:

INTERIOR—MEDIUM SHOT, HIGH, THE LIVING ROOM

We are looking down at Michael on the couch. He has finally dozed off and looks almost peaceful. Cathy enters quietly, looks at him tenderly, is reassured, exits.

Sudden weird sound effect. Michael's right hand twitches violently.

MICHAEL (*in   Charlie ...
anguish*)

Silence. He relaxes into deep sleep again.

INTERIOR—MEDIUM SHOT, THE ELLIS KITCHEN IN CAMBRIDGE

Morning—sunlight floods through the windows. Michael and Cathy, middle-aged again, as at the beginning, are eating bacon and eggs.

CATHY   No pain at all, darling? Really?

MICHAEL   Good as gold. Can hardly believe I
                   had 200 dollars worth of dental
                   surgery yesterday.

They eat silently a moment. Michael looks uneasy.

MICHAEL   Ah ... uh ... Do you remember the earthquake at Cal Tech? Our first night together?

CATHY   Earthquake? What earthquake?

MICHAEL   There was no earthquake that
(*over-eagerly*) night?

CATHY   Of course not. How could I forget a thing like that?

MICHAEL   It *was* the drug then. After the surgery, with the drugs in me, I was remembering my life but it was all mixed up, confused ...

CATHY (*firmly*) I always love fucking with you, my precious Michael, but I've never felt the Earth move. That only happens in Hemingway novels.

NEW ANGLE—CLOSE UP

Michael looks unreasonably relieved at this testimony. Cut to:

EXTERIOR—HARVARD SKYLINE, TRACKING
SHOT

Camera pans down slowly, out of the sky, past trees in flower, to find students on their way to morning classes.

MICHAEL   It wasn't just that I had two sets of
(V.O.)   memories.... Somehow, it was
                 worse than that.... I knew, in some
                 way, that this was only the begin-
                 ning, only the first crack in the fab-
                 ric ...

*In the distance, Michael and Simon walking
together.*

MICHAEL   And I was afraid to talk about it to
(V.O.)   anyone ... even you....

TRACKING SHOT—WE CROSS YARD AND FIND
MICHAEL AND SIMON

Michael and Simon are walking toward us.

SIMON   You're really feeling back to nor-
                 mal?

MICHAEL   I'm in the pink. In the pink, man.
(*imitating*   Ready to take on Rambo.
prizefighter)

SIMON   You mean Rocky. (*Seriously:*) I was
                 worried about the mixture of drugs.
                 I don't want to start another argu-
                 ment, but a guy with rigid beliefs
                 like you can be traumatized by a
                 reframing experience. I mean
                 fucked, flustered, flabbergasted and
                 far from home ...

NEW ANGLE—MEDIUM CLOSE

MICHAEL (*too emphatic*)   Well, you can stop worrying. I'm fine.

They walk a few more steps.

MICHAEL   Uh ... what do you mean "reframing"?

SIMON   It's what happens when the brain gives up one model of reality and starts to build a new model. Any shock or confusion can trigger it. Especially drugs.

MICHAEL (*easily*)   Oh. I guess I did have some reframing yesterday. I couldn't tell which memories were real. I ... sort of drifted out of science into science-fiction. Time travel stuff.... The past was the present. But, really, it's all over. I'm normal again.

They stop, obviously about to head in different directions.

SIMON   Well, keep in touch; if you have any after-effects ...

MICHAEL (*cheerily*)   I'm not about to go yodeling off to the funny farm, Simon. I'm fine.

NEW ANGLE—TRACKING SHOT

They part. The camera follows Michael. Eerie music.

SIMON (*V.O.*)   Reframing. It's what happens when the brain gives up one model of reality and starts to build a new one.

CATHY (*V.O.*)   I've never felt the Earth move.

SIMON (*V.O.*)   Reframing.

CATHY (*V.O.*)   That was quite a tremor last night. Felt like about five on the Richter.

TREE (*V.O.*)   You can have your scientific skepticism, professor. In that case my superstitions saved my life.

LECTURER   Our scientific models are not reality.
(*from the next   They are human maps of reality.
scene, V.O.*)

TREE suddenly appears, coming from a side-path. She is carrying books on psychology this time, not astrology, but is still dressed in a provocative style. She sees Michael, and he stops awkwardly, looking guilty.

TREE   Morning, professor.

MICHAEL   Good morning, Miss Forest.

TREE   Tree. Remember?

Michael laughs with embarassment.

MICHAEL   I'm sorry. Truly. I ... uh ... had dental surgery and the drugs really hit me.

MEDIUM CLOSE SHOT—TREE AND MICHAEL

TREE   Is that all? Or was it remembering
                        you had a wife that really hit you?

Michael is under so much stress that Tree misun-
derstands his expression.

TREE   Look, Professor, don't be afraid of
                        me for Christ's sake. I didn't think
                        you'd leave her and elope with me
                        or something. I know married men,
                        okay? This isn't *Fatal Attraction* ...

MICHAEL   Thank you.... It's not that.... It's
(*showing more of*   the drugs. The dentist's drugs, I
the emotion he   mean ... I don't normally push the
hid from Cathy   envelope ...
and Simon)

TREE (*grinning*)   I know—you only take drugs when
                        you're with a wild, wicked, witchy
                        young girl like me ... and that only
                        happens once a year, right?

MICHAEL   Would you believe twice in thirty
(*wry, but*   years?
regaining
balance)

TREE (*seriously*)   Yeah, I think I'd believe that. You're
                        the type. No mysticism in science,
                        no straying from marriage ... no
                        monkey business anywhere. Mr.
                        Straight Arrow. You're cute in an
                        old-fashioned way. Are you okay?
                        You want me to walk with you?

MICHAEL   You're Simon's girl ...
(*suddenly*)

TREE   I'm nobody's girl. Possessiveness is
                 bad karma.

MICHAEL   Look, I want to sit for a minute and
                 just think. I'll be okay. Honest.
                 Don't worry about me.

TREE   Some people need reality as a crutch
                 because they can't deal with drugs.

MICHAEL   Christ, it's 20 years since I first
(*laughing*)   heard that!

TREE (*looking   I guess you'll be okay ... but Jesus if
him over*)   you feel too spacey go home and
                 just cancel your classes. Will you?

MICHAEL   You gave me a good laugh. I'll be
                 okay ...

*TREE starts to walk off, looks back once with
concern.*

MICHAEL   Can I see you again?

TREE   Only if you're feeling wicked and
                 witchy ...

Her footsteps recede. A bird calls.

MEDIUM SHOT—MICHAEL

*Michael sits on a bench to rest. He lights a ciga-
rette.*

MICHAEL
(V.O.)

Marijuana, Dr. Ellis ... codeine ... sodium pentothol ... adultery.... a girl who believes in karma and tells fortunes with cards ... angels on the telephone ... you may end up meditating and eating eggplant and yogurt, Dr. Ellis ...

Cut to:

INTERIOR LONG SHOT—AN AUDITORIUM

The largest classroom in Cal Tech. About 150 students are listening to a Guest Lecturer.

LECTURER

... and that was how Niels Bohr realized that matter is neither particles nor waves. Particles and waves are just two models that are useful for us to use in physics when we describe matter. We *create* the models. We do not "find" them.

INTERIOR MEDIUM SHOT—NEW ANGLE

We see the young Michael among the students. He is perhaps a year older than in the bedroom flashback with Cathy and has grown a mustache. His hair is less neatly trimmed. His clothing and that of the others makes clear that they are graduate students and becoming more casual, although it is not yet the 60s.

LECTURER
(V.O.)

And the universe is not our equations. Our equations are just useful tools we create to describe the universe.

NEW ANGLE

We see Michael down left, looking at the lecturer. All the other students in this shot (except one) are also looking at the lecturer. The sole exception, who looks older than the other students, is a young man with a tough, intelligent, somewhat brutal face. He is staring at Michael.

LECTURER
(V.O.)

As Korzybski said, the map is not the territory. Our scientific models are not reality. They are human *maps of reality.*

INTERIOR CLOSE-UP—NEW ANGLE

We see the back of Mike's head and neck. Camera moves in closer. Suspense music as we hold on back of Mike's neck.

LECTURER
(V.O.)

This is what is known as the Copenhagen Interpretation of quantum mechanics ...

Michael suddenly turns and looks uneasily behind him.

NEW ANGLE—LONG SHOT

The older student quickly looks away when Mike almost catches him staring.

LECTURER   ... because it was invented in
(*V.O.*)   Copenhagen by Dr. Bohr and his
                  students—although not, as some
                  say, in the Carlsberg brewery....

NEW ANGLE—CLOSE-UP

We pan in on the closed, engimatic face of the older student, which reveals no more than a locked safe.

MICHAEL   I've seen him before.... No, I met
(*V.O.*)   him later ... I mean ...

EXTERIOR—PANNING SHOT, ROME

The camera moves at dizzying speed down a street in Rome and suddenly shows the Coliseum looming in the distance. Cut to:

EXTERIOR—LONG SHOT, TWILIGHT

A high hill framed by a glorious sunset. On top of the hill we see the grim outlines of three crosses. Cut to:

EXTERIOR—CLOSE-UP

The human hand again. We hear the hammer strike the nail and as the nail sinks into the hand, red blood gushes. We hear the terrible scream of the crucified man.

YOUTHFUL   Dr. Ellis! Dr. Ellis!
VOICE (*V.O.*)

Cut to:

EXTERIOR—HARVARD YARD, MEDIUM SHOT

Michael is sitting on the bench, deep in reverie. A male student wearing the SSA lightning bolts is approaching. He is blonde and tall and blue-eyed and something about him suggests an idealistic young Nazi.

STUDENT   Dr. Ellis?

Michael looks up, his eyes coming a long, long way back.

MICHAEL   Oh, Carl. I just sat down to enjoy
                 the spring air. Am I late for class?

CARL (*looking   Not yet, sir. Could I walk along
at his wrist   with you? I wanted to ask you
watch*)   something ... if I may, sir?

SAME—NEW ANGLE, TRACKING SHOT

Michael and Carl start to walk across the campus.

CARL   It's about the astrology investiga-
                 tion, sir. There's a lot of scuttlebutt
                 going around ...

MICHAEL   And what does the scuttlebutt say?
(*easily, with no
defensiveness*)

CARL (*nervous*) Well, some guys in the print shop
                 claim to have seen Dr. Selene's

report. They say he *supports* astrology

MICHAEL   Not exactly. But his data does tend to "support" one aspect of astrological prediction. We will need more studies, of course, but—

CARL (*leaning close, lowering his voice*)   Do you think Dr. Selene fudged the data?

MICHAEL (*shocked*)   Simon? Good God, he wouldn't do a thing like that.

Carl leans even closer, and leers.

CARL   Aw, come on, doc. You told us at the last SSA meeting those psychic and occult people always fake what they do.

Michael stares at Carl with growing dismay, recognizing a mirror image of his own former dogmatism. Slow fade.

INTERIOR—LONG SHOT, THE ELLIS
BEDROOM. NIGHT.

Cathy is sleeping soundly. Michael creeps out of bed, quietly, checks that she is asleep and tiptoes from the room.

INTERIOR—TRACKING SHOT. THE STAIRS.

Michael is still tiptoeing as he heads down to the living room.

INTERIOR—LIVING ROOM, MEDIUM CLOSE

Michael sits at his home computer and begins typing on the keyboard.

INTERIOR—CLOSE UP OF SCREEN ON
COMPUTER CONSOLE

We see the following words:

MY TWO LIVES.
LOCK IN.
RETREIVAL CODE: DEATH OF GOD TOP SECRET

INTERIOR—MEDIUM SHOT, MICHAEL AT THE
COMPUTER

Michael is typing rapidly, unloading his pent-up anxieties.

MICHAEL   Either I am mad or reincarnation is
(V.O.)   true—and things even more
                 unthinkable than reincarnaton are
                 true also. The Guardians or Custo-
                 dians of this planet displaced me in
                 time after I killed Christ ...

Cut to:

INTERIOR—AN AUDITORIUM AT CAL TECH

Long panning shot shows a room packed with students. At the podium, incongruously dressed in a

Roman toga, is a middle-aged scientist, Dr. Abraham Baum. His speech reveals a man who knows as much about oratory as about physics. Behind him on the wall is a large blow-up photo of Dr. J. Robert Oppenheimer.

DR. BAUM (*earnestly*)	Of course, some people say to me, "Dr. Baum, stick to physics. That's what you understand. Leave politics to the politicians."

Camera pans over the audience. Many young faces, painfully grappling with the problem that besets the speaker.

DR. BAUM (V.O.)	But my answer is that the world got into this mess because we left it to the politicians. They have no concept of what the bomb means. They don't grasp what fallout means to people thousands of miles from a nuclear explosion. They are like little children playing with loaded revolvers.

We find young Michael in the audience: he has added a small goatee to his mustache and his hair is longer. He is bored and climbing over others' feet as he attempts to leave inconspicuously.

NEW ANGLE

We move in medium close on Dr. Baum, in ordinary modern business suit.

DR. BAUM   And while the little children play
(*passionately*)   with their loaded guns, we who
                  know the danger have a duty to
                  speak out. Others may hide under
                  rocks and tremble with fear of the
                  bogey man or Senator McCarthy
                  but I tell you ...

                  NEW ANGLE—THE AUDIENCE

*Medium close shot of Michael reaching the end of
the row and about to leave. The student who
stared at Mike earlier leans forward and whispers
angrily.*

STUDENT   Why won't you listen to the man?

MICHAEL   Peace, brother. Watch all events
(*ironically*)   with dispassion.

*We hear Dr. Baum's passionate voice as we fade
out. His last sentence carries over a bit to the next
scene.*

DR. BAUM (*a   Scientists are not exempt from the
voice crying in   moral burden of all men. We must
the wilderness*)   think. We must choose. We must
                   take responsibility.

        INTERIOR TRACKING SHOT: A PIZZERIA

*Close up of a headline on a newspaper, with
Baum's photo:*

McCARTHY CALLS BAUM "RED AGENT"

*Camera is panning even as we read this and we see
paper is in hand of the older student with the hard,
intelligent face (Peter Stone) who watched Michael
in the lecture scene and spoke in the Baum scene.
We are in a pizzeria in Cambridge. All the students
are doing graduate work and are somewhat older.
We find Mike and Cathy at a table with friends and
move in to medium close on them.*

*Mike now has longer hair and a stragglier goatee.
Cathy is in jeans. One of their friends already has a
full beard. On the juke box we hear Chuck Berry.
On the wall is a blow-up of Bogart with drooping
cigarette from* Casablanca.

MALE
STUDENT #1
(*a bit drunk*)

The fuck you say. I'm telling you the Copenhagen Interpretation was brilliant enough for its time, but now it's just an excuse for intellectual laziness. We should stop quoting old man Bohr as dogma and think about what the goddamn equations *mean.*

MICHAEL
(*with the irony
we begin to
recognize as
typical of him*)

Are you talking physics or are you talking philosophy? I'm finding it hard enough to get my Ph.D. in physics. I don't want to work on one in philosophy at the same time.

NEW ANGLE—THE SAME TABLE

Male Student #2 is examining the pizza suspiciously.

MALE
STUDENT #1

Good old pragmatic Michael.
Never ask what anything means,
just ask if it works. Right?

MICHAEL
(*lighting
cigarette*)

Pragmatism was good enough for
Bohr. It was good enough for Bridg-
man. It was good enough for
Heisenberg.

CATHY (*also a
little drunk; to
the tune of "That
Old Time
Religion"*)

Give me that old time pragmatic

That old time pragmatic

It was good for Bohr and Bridgman

It was good for Bohr and Bridgman

And it's good enough for me.

MALE
STUDENT #2
(*over Cathy*)

Hey, I think we got anchovies on
this pizza.

FEMALE
STUDENT #2
(*over Male
Student #2*)

Michael, haven't you ever once
wondered what an electron is *really*
doing when we're not looking at it?

MICHAEL
(*cool and a bit
superior*)

Yes, I did wonder about that when I
was a freshman. Then I realized
Heisenberg was right. Wondering
about that is like wondering how
many angels can dance on the head
of a pin. It's philosophy, not science.

FEMALE
STUDENT #1

And what's the difference between
philosophy and science, Mr. Expert,
when we get down to basics?

MICHAEL	Science is what we know. Philosophy is what we don't know and can only guess about.
FEMALE STUDENT #2	Einstein wondered about what those electrons are doing when we can't see them.
MALE STUDENT #1 (*speaking over her*)	Either the electrons only exist in our heads, which is solipsism, or the electrons are doing *somefuckingthing* even when we're not looking at them.
MALE STUDENT #2	You all know I can't *stand anchovies on my goddam pizza.*
FEMALE STUDENT #2 (*to Michael*)	Don't you ever ask yourself, "In all these equations we handle so neatly, what the hell is real? Really real?"
MICHAEL (*imitating scene from* Treasure of the Sierra Madre)	I am a quantum physicist. I don't got to show you no steeeenking reality.

NEW ANGLE—SAME TABLE

Everybody laughs at Mike's Mexican dialect. Other figures in 1950s college clothing pass going to or from the bathrooms.

MALE STUDENT #1	But I want to *know*, some day, what the fuckin' electrons do with their time when we're not observing them.

MICHAEL (*drily*)	I want to have a fat bank account and take crap from nobody.
FEMALE STUDENT #2	The Schrödinger equations actually do tell us what the electrons are doing when we're not peeking. They're only in one state when we look, right? Well, then,when we don't look, they're in every possible state.
MICHAEL	Oh, Jesus, that's really confusing the map with the territory.
FEMALE STUDENT #2	You don't keep up with the journals, my friend. Hugh Everett, down at Princeton, just proved it. The electrons are in every mathematically possible *eigenstate* up till the exact nanosecond when we bombard them with light to see what the little buggers are up to ...
MALE STUDENT #2	None of you are listening. They put goddam anchovies on the pizza. You promised me. "No goddam anchovies."
MALE STUDENT #1 (*skeptically, to Female #2*)	Yeah, and Schrödinger's cat is dead and alive at the same time. And Hitler remained a house painter in some universes. Jesus, I'm asking for realism in physics, not surrealism.

FEMALE STUDENT #2	Look at the damned equations again. The classic fuckin Erwin Schrödinger wave equations we use every day.
MICHAEL (*to Male #1*)	That's what happens when you ask about reality in physics. You'll get a cuckoo answer. Put money in thy purse, as the fellow said.

A man in a Roman Army uniform suddenly passes the table. Michael, startled, looks after this apparition in total confusion. The others do not notice.

CATHY (*singing again*)	It was good for old von Neumann It was good for old von Neumann And it's good enough for me.

Her last line carries over as we cut quickly to:

INTERIOR—ROOM IN ROMAN BARRACKS, JERUSALEM

Near sunset. Long shadows dominate the room, where we see a middle-aged Jew, thin and scrawny, stripped naked, hanging from wall-chains. His back is to us, and he wears a crown of thorns. A soldier is systematically flogging him with a whip. Camera abruptly pans back and we see Michael, in officer's uniform. He is lounging, half-sitting on a table, perhaps unhappy but looking bored. He is the officer in charge of torturing the Jew. The Jew screams with terrible pain as we cut to:

EXTERIOR—A CAFE IN MEXICO

Midday in Cuernavaca. The sun burns down on a group of tables at which American tourists sit, panting, trying to quench their thirst. Camera pans to the table where Mike and Cathy are sitting with Peter Stone, the "older student" who once stared at Mike in physics class. Mike now has a beard. Cathy has love beads and a headband. At a nearby table a portable radio blares The Beatles, "I Want To Hold Your Hand." Peter Stone is talking very earnestly to Mike and Cathy.

PETER STONE   The space game came to an end, the time game came to an end and then the Peter Stone game came to an end. I was in eternity except that there was no "I."

SAME TABLE—NEW ANGLE

MICHAEL   What the *hell* kind of mushroom was that, Peter?

PETER STONE   The Indians call it *teonanacatl.* That means "the flesh of God."

CATHY   Sounds dangerous to me. God only knows what a chemical like that might do to your brain.

PETER STONE   There's a big research project on
(with missionary   this back at Harvard right now.
zeal)   They haven't found any bad side-effects.

MICHAEL   Harvard? I *knew* you looked famil-
                           iar. Didn't I see you in a physics
                           class there once?

PETER STONE   No, I've never been at Harvard. I'm
(immediately,   a Cornell man, myself.
smoothly, with
the face of a
practiced and
plausible liar)

CATHY (*not*   Who's doing this research at Har-
hiding her   vard, Pete? We might know them.
skepticism)

Camera moves in on Michael. He has taken his
wallet out and is separating his U.S. from Mexican
money. His face changes. He is vaguely alarmed.

PETER STONE   Three psychologists. Uh named uh
(*V.O.*)   Metzner and Alpert and uh um yes
                           a guy named Leary.

CLOSE-UP: TIGHT ON TABLE TOP

Weird, unearthly music. We see two piles of
money. On top of one is the eye above a pyramid
on the American dollar. On top of the other is the
bell above a pyramid on the Mexican peso.

CATHY (*V.O.*)   Oh? "*Theory* Leary." We've met
                           him. He's trying to turn psychology
                           into a branch of physics. (*Imitating*
                           Dr. Leary's speech:) "Where are the
                           bodies in space-time?"

TIGHT CLOSE-UP ON DOLLAR

Music grows frantic as we pan in on the eye above the pyramid.

CATHY (*V.O., still imitating Leary*)	"Don't talk to me about neurosis or adjustment. Where are the bodies in space-time? What signals are they exchanging?" Old Theory Leary.

TIGHT CLOSE-UP ON PESO

Frantic music as we pan in on the bell above the pyramid.

PETER STONE (*V.O.*)	Well, if consciousness is chemical, chemicals can change consciousness, right?

EXTERIOR MEDIUM SHOT—SAME SCENE

Neither Cathy nor Peter notice that Michael is having some sort of anxiety attack.

PETER STONE	I mean, suppose normal consciousness screens out some of the most important signals we should be receiving? Suppose this mushroom really does expand consciousness by opening the brain to new signals? Then we'd perceive a new reality.
CATHY	But suppose it poisons you in the long run, Peter?

TIGHT CLOSE-UP ON THE DOLLAR

The camera moves in again on the eye above the pyramid, more rapidly than in previous similar shot. Spooky music. Quick cut to:

TIGHT CLOSE-UP ON THE PESO

Rapid zoom-lens close-up of the bell above the pyramid.

PETER STONE
(*V.O.*)

The Indians here have been using *teonanacatl* for thousands of years with no bad effects.

EXTERIOR MEDIUM SHOT—THE TABLE. NEW ANGLE

CATHY
(*cynically*)

They don't seem to be models of industry or rationality exactly.

PETER STONE
(*earnestly, but with a hint of con-man*)

Industry and rationality are not the whole of what humans need to be and know. There are intuitive kinds of knowlege our society may desparately need, Mrs. Ellis. Our power is so fucking great already. We may need wisdom, too, before we—

He is interrupted by a sudden crash. Michael has fainted and fallen over, dragging his chair down with the dead weight of his body. Cathy and Peter jump up and kneel over Michael, and there is a sudden, unearthly shriek.

EXTERIOR—LONG SHOT OF CAFE

A buzzard is flying by overhead, making the shrieking noise.

EXTERIOR—MEDIUM CLOSE SHOT

Cathy is holding Michael's head in her lap. She wets a cloth from the water on the table and wipes his brow. On soundtrack, we hear chanting voices begin.

VOICES (V.O.)   One! Two! Three! Four!

EXTERIOR LONG PANNING SHOT—HARVARD
YARD

A riot is occurring. Cops are clubbing students. Tear-gas haze whirls over everything. Camera jumps and bobs uneasily, as in newsreel.

VOICES OF   We don't want your fucking war!
STUDENTS (in   Five! Six! Seven! Eight! Organize to
chorus)   smash the State! Hey, hey, LBJ—
                   how many kids did you kill today?

EXTERIOR MEDIUM CLOSE—SCIENCE
BUILDING

We see Michael, now in his mid-30s, scuttling to get into Science Building and avoid the violence. He has a neat beard and the casual tweeds that seem obligatory for Full Professors. In the background we hear the student proctors beginning again.

STUDENTS   One! Two! Three! Four! We don't
(*V.O., chanting*)   want your fucking war!

INTERIOR MEDIUM CLOSE—INSIDE SCIENCE
BUILDING

Michael and another professor walking down hall.

PROFESSOR   I never imagined anything like this
                  could happen at Harvard.

MICHAEL   The whole country is wigging out.
                  Why should we be immune?

PROFESSOR   But Harvard students....! In my
                  day, they were all gentlemen.

They walk a moment in silence.

PROFESSOR   How's Charlie?

MICHAEL   Still in Vietnam. He's made second
                  lieutenant.

He nods a farewell and opens a door to find:

INTERIOR—THE SENATE IN ROME

*Dr. Baum in toga again stands in the speaker's
position in the center and is orating.*

DR. BAUM   Weapons that only a madman
                  would use, or even contemplate
                  using. Weapons that wage genetic
                  warfare against unborn genera-
                  tions. Weapons of genocide.

Michael looks only vaguely confused, not flabbergasted. His mind does not quite take in the incredible thing he is seeing.

MICHAEL   Oh, pardon me. I must have the
                 wrong room.

INTERIOR MEDIUM LONG—THE HALLWAY

Michael closes door and backs up. He looks more confused, not less.

INTERIOR LONG SHOT—ROMAN BARRACKS:
JERUSALEM

The soldier is still whipping the Jew. Michael in his Harvard tweeds is lounging where Michael in Roman officer's uniform lounged before. The whip falls methodically four times.

EXTERIOR—LONG SHOT OF HILL IN
JERUSALEM

The three crosses starkly outlined against the rose-ated sunset.

VOICE (*in*   My God, My God ...
agony)

EXTERIOR—MEDIUM LONG: SAME HILL

The Jew we saw being whipped is on the middle cross. It is he who is crying out.

THE JEW   Why have you forsaken me?
(*passionately*)

EXTERIOR—MEDIUM CLOSE: SAME HILL

Michael, now in proper Centurion uniform, looks disturbed. He begins to draw his sword. A subaltern deferentially but firmly puts his hand on Michael's arm.

SUBALTERN   You're gonna get in trouble for that one of these days, sir.

MICHAEL   There's a limit to everything, for
(*firmly*)   God's sake. This man has suffered enough.

SAME—NEW ANGLE, MEDIUM LONG SHOT

As Michael starts forward, drawing his sword, an angry old woman In the crowd throws a rotten tomato at the Jew on the middle cross. It hits him in the face.

THE JEW   God forgive them. They don't know what they're doing.

Michael steps forward and firmly, professionally, thrusts his sword into the Jew's heart. Angry outburst from the crowd, who wanted to see the victim suffer longer. Blood spurts onto Michael's uniform.

SAME—TIGHT CLOSE-UP FROM GROUND
LEVEL

We see Michael staring at the blood on his hand with some horror. Hand dominates shot; Michael's face is above and behind hand. From out of his

mouth comes a long, low howl of terror, far
beyond what a trained military officer would
express at the mere sight of blood. He seems to
know something he does not want to know. The
voice cracks at last into a choked sob overlapping
our fade to:

INTERIOR—SIMON'S KITCHEN. MEDIUM
SHOT

Simon and Michael are sitting at the table. A bottle
of whiskey now stands between the empty coffee
cups and Simon raises it with an enquiring expres-
sion. Michael nods and Simon pours whiskey into
each cup.

Outside the window, we see the first cinnamon
streaks of dawn. Michael takes his whiskey in a
gulp and shudders. Simon sips a bit, stretches his
arms and finally speaks, kindly and without mock-
ery.

SIMON   The man who killed Christ.... Well,
                         it's something new. But why is it
                         that everytime I meet a reincarna-
                         tion case they were somebody
                         important in their last life?

Michael looks surprised and a bit confused.

SIMON   I meet people who were Cleopatra
(philosophically)   ... or Napoleon ... or even Marilyn
                         Monroe lately.... I never meet any-
                         body who was *un*important the last
                         time around....

MICHAEL
(*wearily*)

You don't understand.... This is all what you call "screen memory."

SIMON
(*surprised that Michael knows the term*)

Screen memory? You figured that out on your own? You don't need a psychologist ... maybe you should be a psychologist.

MICHAEL
(*impatiently*)

You explained screen memory to me at an SSA meeting .... we were discussing auto accidents with UFO reports, remember? You explained that anybody can have a false memory after a shock or trauma. To replace what they can't really remember. You said it's more common than amnesia.

SIMON

So then you didn't literally kill Christ?

Michael shudders and pours more whiskey. He drinks in a gulp.

MICHAEL
(*very calm at first, his voice gradually rising*)

Not literally ... but every physicist in the world has collaborated in that murder ... for forty years and more now. All we do is ask for more and more money to create more and more explosive power and (*voice cracks*) deliver the bombs over longer and longer distances ... in shorter and shorter times ... to kill more and more peo-

ple. What a wonderful use of
human intelligence ... (*almost sobs*)

*Pause. Simon watches sympathetically. Mike pulls
himself together.*

SIMON (*mildly*)   Wow.... How long have you been
                         holding that in?

MICHAEL   Most of my adult life.

NEW ANGLE

Pause, then Simon speaks.

SIMON   But there's more ... something
               behind the screen memory ...

MICHAEL   Yes.... This is where you really have
                 to tell me if I'm going off my
                 skull....

EXTERIOR: TWILIGHT; THE 3 CROSSES ON
THE HILL

Thunder strikes and lightning flashes.

CLOSE-UP—MICHAEL

*He watches the rain washing the blood off his
hands.*

MICHAEL'S   All religions are equally true to the
FATHER (*V.O.*)   masses ...

His voice continues as we cut to:

EXTERIOR—A CROWDED STREET IN ROME

FATHER (continued)	... equally false to the philosopher, and equally useful to the politician. Dear boy, all of this is terribly embarassing to me but what can I do? I am a Senator; I must obey protocol.

Cattle, donkeys, chariots, masses of people and a general sense of noise and filth dominate as camera pans over street and finds Michael, still in uniform, and his father, in a toga.

MICHAEL	I understand, father.
FATHER	Do you? I wonder. After five years service in the Provinces you hardly seem like a Roman anymore.
MICHAEL (*cryptically*)	One sees many odd things in the Provinces.
FATHER	I hope you are not so naive as to believe what you see, dear boy. The eyes are great deceivers. Whoever said "seeing is believing" was a fool. And you *are* imaginative.
MICHAEL	Please don't start that all over again, father.

EXTERIOR: PATIO OF THE SYBILLINE ORACLE

Michael and Father are now under a shaded roof, although still outside the building proper.

FATHER
(*strictly*)

You were 12 years old when you told your mother that absurd story. A god speaking to you! And I think you believed it.

MICHAEL

The Jews hear their god speaking all the time. Or some of them do. One man I crucified ...

FATHER

Please, dear boy, spare me the details. Officially, we are there to civilize them. I would rather not know the specifics. It would undermine my sincerity when I speak in the Senate. I am supposed to believe we do nothing but good for the people whose lands we occupy.

SAME—NEW ANGLE

Michael looks at his father with baffled affection and increased curiosity.

MICHAEL

You don't really believe in anything, do you, father?

FATHER

Of course, I do. A man who believes nothing is as much a fool as a man who believes everything. I believe I would like to remain in the Senate for the rest of my life. I believe bringing my son here to the Sybilline oracle will undermine those shameful rumors that I am an Atheist. I believe that the universe consists of atoms and the void, as Democritus taught. And I would like to believe you are old enough and sane enough not to take it into your head to put any confidence in what the Oracle tells you. She is a crazy woman and under the influence of dreadful drugs all the time.

MICHAEL
(*patiently*)

Just what am I supposed to ask this drug-maddened woman?

FATHER

Oh, whatever you choose, dear boy. Ask if you will be successful in love. (As if any man ever is....) Ask if you will become a General soon. Ask anything but do not be naïve enough to believe what she tells you. Gods do not talk to us. All that exists ...

MICHAEL

... is atoms and the void. I'll remember. I first heard you say that when I was twelve. At the time of the ... incident.

FATHER

It is worth repeating. Atoms and the void, dear boy. All else is speculation—that is to say, mere fantasy.

MICHAEL

There is just one thing, father ...

FATHER

Yes?

MICHAEL   I have never seen those marvelous
                 atoms, but I have heard a god speak
                 to me.

We hear a weird cackle of laughter as we cut to:

INTERIOR—MEDIUM SHOT; THE SYBILLINE
ORACLE

The scene appears lit by fires burning below the floor. Clouds of smoke from the burning herbs fill the room. Shadows dance on the walls, making monstrous shapes. Gradually we make out the whirling, deliriously dancing figure of the Oracle. She is quite old and stunningly ugly.

ORACLE   The young man comes to the
                 woman old. The young man speaks
                 in accents bold. "Oh, when shall I
                 find mine own true love? The wrath
                 of the gods still lurks above."

SAME—NEW ANGLE

MICHAEL   Priestess of Sybil, priestess of my
(with painful ancestors, priestess of She whose
childish   secret name is Isis, tell me true: Did
simplicity, not a god ever speak to me?
wearing any
mask of
protective irony)

SAME—NEW ANGLE

Medium shot of Michael and Oracle. She sways in half-dance.

ORACLE
(*schizophrenic
babble*)

Aye, aye, a god did speak to thee,
and thou did kill a god.

MICHAEL
(*frightened, but
indignant*)

I did never kill a god, if such were
possible. I swear it.

ORACLE
(*dancing away*)

Aye, aye, thou didst kill a god
unknown, a god knocking on the
door of time. (*Singing:*) And now
the Empire ne'er shall end, till thou
shallst make that god thy friend.
(*Screaming:*) Look to thy hand! Thy
hand!

SPECIAL EFFECT

*A nuclear bomb goes off in the distance. We see the
mushroom cloud and then we see White Light
bouncing off the screen to illuminate theatre. Cut
to:*

EXTERIOR—MEDIUM SHOT, BUNKER

*Michael and other scientists, with protective gog-
gles, are observing the nuclear blast. We are perhaps at the Nevada test center. Michael looks as he
did in his mid-30s, i.e. in the Harvard riot
sequence. The screen is bleached and whitish from
the blast.*

UNIDENTIFIED
SCIENTIST
(*Hal Holbrook
type*)

It always make me think of what
Oppenheimer said. Now science
knows the meaning of sin.

MICHAEL	That's the silliest damned thing the old man ever said.
UNIDENTIFIED SCIENTIST (*startled, defensive*)	Oh, you're like Teller? You really believe in this?
MICHAEL (*impatient, as if explaining to a child*)	One country is going to be superior in the world, always. As long as I live here, I want it to be America. (*Ironically:*) That's mere pragmatism, of course, but I have no head for theology.
UNIDENTIFIED SCIENTIST (*sadly*)	And our universities are turning out more barbarians like you every year.

LONG SHOT—THE DESERT

The mushroom cloud slowly spreading and then slowly dispersing.

SIMON (*V.O.*)	Did you believe all that when you said it?
MICHAEL (*V.O.*)	Simon, I've never said what I really think, or shown my real self … I've always been afraid of what people would do if they suspected who I am …. or what I am….

INTERIOR—THE ORACLE OF SYBIL

The Sybil is no longer an ugly old woman. She is TREE, in a translucent and very sexy set of veils.

MICHAEL (*frightened, but indignant*)	I did never kill a god, if such were possible. I swear it.
TREE (*dancing away*)	Aye, aye, thou didst kill a god unknown, a god knocking on the door of time. (*Singing:*) And now the Empire ne'er shall end, till thou shallst make that god thy friend.
MICHAEL	The Empire shall never end ... ?
TREE (*screaming*)	Look to thy future! Look!

Michael stares in horror at something offscreen.

LONG TRACKING SHOT—SLOW MOTION

A military funeral somewhere in the U.S. Flag-draped coffin borne by Honor Guard. "Taps" played very slowly and mournfully. Cut to:

MEDIUM INTERIOR SHOT—SIMON'S KITCHEN

The whiskey bottle is near empty now. Full dawn shines in the window.

MICHAEL	I remembered it all as a child. But then I lost it, of course.
SIMON	You mean you stopped remembering?

MICHAEL   I had to. I was afraid of going crazy.
                 I couldn't talk. (*Almost weeping for
                 a second.*) I couldn't talk. When I
                 realized it wasn't really an angel.

SIMON   This was at the time of the phone
                 calls? When you were twelve?

MICHAEL   No, later. At Cal Tech. The night
                 Cathy and I first slept together. Is
                 that Freudian enough for you?

SIMON   We don't have to worry about
                 Freud here. Do you want to tell me
                 about it?

NEW ANGLE—CLOSE-UP ON MICHAEL

MICHAEL   We had been dating for nearly a
                 year. No sex. Well, some petting. It
                 was back in the '50s, you know. I
                 finally got her into bed ...

Fade to:

INTERIOR—THE STUDENT BEDROOM AT CAL
                 TECH

*Mike and Cathy are in bed. He is caressing her
under the sheets.*

CATHY (*panting*   That creatures who claim to be
a bit)   angels may be devils ... demons
                          from hell—trying enter you and ...

MICHAEL   Enter *me*? And?

CATHY   Oh, darling, darling ...
(*control lost*)

MICHAEL   Cathy ... Cathy ... I love you ...
(*V.O.*)

Quick cut to:

SPECIAL EFFECT

The door to the bedroom bursts open. Weird, shrieking music—the same note repeated at higher and higher decibel levels in the following super-quick cuts. (Editing at the speed of the shower scene in Psycho.*)*

LONG SHOT—MIKE'S P.O.V.

The music shrieks as the outline of a bald dwarf appears in the doorway.

LONG SHOT—THE BEDROOM

Mike and Cathy sitting up in bed, terrified, as the dwarf rushes at superhuman speed across the room to the bed.

LONG SHOT—MIKE'S P.O.V.

The music shrieks three times as two more dwarfs appear in the doorway, then disappear as they race into the room, then are replaced by three dwarfs in the doorway.

LONG SHOT—THE BEDROOM

A dozen dwarfs running across the room as music shrieks.

CLOSE SHOT—THE BED

Cathy is in shock or in trance; her eyes are glazed and she sees nothing. Mike is struggling to climb out of bed and up the wall as insectoid dwarfish hands grab at his arms and legs.

TIGHT CLOSE-UP ON MIKE

Terrible shriek as the abominable instrument is shoved under Mike's right eyelid and pushed up into his brain.

SUBJECTIVE SHOT—MIKE'S P.O.V.

An expressionless bald dwarf shoving the weird instrument toward the camera. Framing of shot should recall exactly Mike's previous vision of the bald dentist using this tool.

SPECIAL EFFECT

Two bars of Beethoven's "Ode to Joy" as we see Michael, in his pajamas, flying through the air. Below him, the buildings of Cal Tech. Above, a great white globe of light toward which he is accelerating.

INTERIOR—A GEODESIC ROOM

White light bathes a circular room in which Michael, naked, is being strapped to a table.

Dwarfs bustle about, all busy with various instruments and unearthly machines.

CLOSE-UP OF MICHAEL

He is half screaming and half weeping, totally terrified

CLOSE-UP—MIKE'S CROTCH

Dwarfish hands are adjusting a machine above Mike's groin. We see enough to gather that his penis is being forcibly inserted into the machine.

CLOSE-UP OF MICHAEL

He is both screaming and weeping, but then his face contorts with involuntary pleasure and further terror.

MEDIUM CLOSE SHOT

The dwarfs are removing the machine from Mike's groin and evidently removing the sperm into a test-tube.

SPECIAL EFFECT

The spiral of the galaxy turning. Four more bars of Beethoven's "Ode to Joy."

MEDIUM LONG SHOT—THE CAL TECH
BEDROOM

Mike and Cathy, both glazed over and entranced, sitting like zombies. The furniture gradually stops jumping up and down. When silence is complete, Mike and Cathy are still staring vacantly into space. The silence continues 10 seconds and we fade to:

MEDIUM SHOT—THE ELLIS LIVING ROOM

Michael, middle-aged again, sitting at the computer typing these memories, or hallucinations.

MICHAEL   It was as if the curtain raised a little
(V.O.)   bit more each time I looked ... and
                 more of what I saw was unbeliev-
                 able ...

SPECIAL EFFECT

We hear the first notes of Beethoven's "Ode to Joy."

Through a warped lens we see events in a large scientific laboratory. All the scientists are speaking Russian, but the sound is slurred and the camera tilts drunkenly from one part of the room to another. Those in the audience who speak Russian hear such fragments as:

FIRST RUSSIAN   ... only when Mars is rising in Tau-
VOICE   rus ...

SECOND   ... it requires a six-dimensional time
RUSSIAN   tunnel ...
VOICE

THIRD   ... up there. But are they our
RUSSIAN   friends?
VOICE

NEW ANGLE

We see the center of all the activity. Two women and a man, all civilian and ordinary-looking Russians, are wired up with electronic equipment monitoring their brain waves. They are facing a wall on which several slides of Cro-Magnon cave art are being projected, starting with the cave painting of the hunters killing the bison that Michael has already seen. Each picture is held on screen one half-second only and in five seconds we see 10 bits of 30,000-year old Cave Art.

Cut to:

INTERIOR—ELLIS LIVING ROOM: CLOSE-UP

Michael sits up, turns from the computer, eyes wide open.

Cut to:

INTERIOR, SUBJECTIVE SHOT—MICHAEL'S
P.O.V.

On the wall of the room, the last three bits of Cave Art are appearing rapidly. Suddenly they are replaced by 10 bits of ancient Egyptian art, each one projected for one half-second only. The "Ode to Joy" continues. Cut to:

INTERIOR, A GEODESIC ROOM—WHITE
LIGHT OVER ALL

Blurry and barely visible in the white glare, a group of the dwarfs from Michael's Cal Tech vision are busy with some complicated apparatus. Gradually, we realize that three of the dwarfs are making "sketches" in the air with some incomprehensible instrument. They are receiving what the three Russian psychics are transmitting. The sketches in the air are being captured by a computeroid machine which is evidently "storing" them in memory. We see the last three specimens of Egyptian art being received and then the first four specimens of ancient Oriental art.

Cut to:

INTERIOR—ELLIS LIVING ROOM, LONG SHOT

The "Ode to Joy" is continuing and mounting in power. Michael is staggering and blundering around in a room totally transformed. Oriental art is now being replaced by 10 specimens of African art, which appear simultaneously on all the walls, for half a second each.

INTERIOR—THE RUSSIAN LABORATORY

The psychics are concentrating on 10 specimens of Classic Greek Art, including the Victory of Samothrace.

INTERIOR TRACKING SHOT—ELLIS
STAIRWAY, LIVING ROOM

Michael is stumbling around, outside "up" and "down" and "right" and "left."

MICHAEL   Russians. I saw Russians. *They're* doing this.

On all walls are images, still coming one per half-second, of Roman art, later Oriental and Byzantine art, medieval art.

SPECIAL EFFECT

The art images now appear alone; even the bare outlines of the Ellis living room have disappeared. Michael is floating amid a whirlwind of 20 classic Rennaisance paintings, one per half-second, for 10 seconds. Beethoven's music is pulsing at the audience in Dolby stereo. The effect is that something more than great art and great music is being transmitted, something art and music only symbolize. Michael floats through 10 seconds of 20 Impressionist paintings, 10 seconds of 20 Van Gogh paintings, 10 seconds of 20 Picasso paintings, 10 seconds of miscellaneous modern art culminating in 3 seconds of 3 sprawling Jackson Pollocks. We hear the conclusion of the "Ode to Joy."

INTERIOR—THE GEODESIC ALL-WHITE ROOM

The dwarfs are turning off various instruments. One speaks

DWARF   Kral lamec melas tropwen.

SECOND   Kral lamec Irpac oroblram.
DWARF

The lights dim. The dwarfish figures, indistinct because of excess light, are now equally indistinct as light fades to darkness. Cut to

INTERIOR—THE ELLIS LIVING ROOM

Michael, in his pajamas, slumped in an easy chair. His face is ecstatic.

MICHAEL
(*V.O., with religious awe*)

Those Russian sons of bitches. They knew all along ... Russians and extraterrestrials ... working together ...

Slowly he rises and turns on a lamp. He walks across the room, still in a daze of mystic euphoria.

INSERT

Michaelangelo's Pieta *held on screen for shortest time in which audience can recognize it.*

INTERIOR—ELLIS LIVING ROOM

Michael walking, smiling.

INSERT

Van Gogh's Starry Sky *held on screen with equal brevity.*

INTERIOR—ELLIS LIVING ROOM

Michael exits through hall door.

INTERIOR—ELLIS BATHROOM

Michael takes some of the sedative pills from the medicine chest, runs water into a glass.

LONG SHOT—THE MILITARY FUNERAL

Over the sound of "Taps" we hear a woman weeping.

INTERIOR—ELLIS BATHROOM

Michael drops the glass and pills.

SPECIAL EFFECT

Aztec calendar slowly spinning. Weird mechanical-musical noises.

EXTERIOR—THE CAFE IN CUERNAVACA,
MEXICO

The sun again burns down on a group of tables at which American tourists sit, panting, trying to quench their thirst. Mike and Cathy are having the same conversation with Peter Stone. The radio in the background is not playing The Beatles but Bing Crosby singing "If You Want To Swing On A Star."

PETER STONE   Suppose this mushroom really does expand consciousness by opening the brain to new signals? Then we'd perceive a new reality.

MICHAEL   Yeah, I can see what you mean.
                     This is like discovering a new scien-
                     tific instrument, a brain telescope.

Cathy registers astonishment and consternation.

PETER STONE   You got it. It's like a genetic mem-
                     ory bank.

MICHAEL   Christ, I'd like to try it.

CATHY   Michael! You can't be serious.

MICHAEL   Why not? We never learn anything
                     without experiment.

CATHY   But this is almost like a drug, isn't
                     it?

PETER STONE   Body drugs have revolutionized
(*very much the*   medicine time and again. Mind
pitchman now)   drugs will probably revolutionize
                     our whole concept of reality.

*He takes a cellophane bag from his pocket and
puts it on the table. Michael stares with fascina-
tion.*

PETER STONE   Four to six of these will change
                     your whole concept of space and
                     time. No research physicist should
                     pass up the chance ...

CATHY   Michael, you can't seriously con-
(*frightened*)   sider this ...

Michael grabs four mushrooms and swallows them, with a grin of boyish adventure we have never seen on him. He quickly swallows some tequila to wash down the "flesh of the gods."

CATHY (*angry*)   For Christ sake, Mike, come back to the hotel. I want to look for that doctor we met yesterday, in case anything goes wrong ...

MICHAEL   Nothing is happening. I feel per-
(*abashed*)   fectly normal.

Cathy watches him with anxiety. Peter waits smugly.

MICHAEL   What is this, Peter? Are you some
(*turning*   kind of Put On Artist?
suspicious)

PETER   Listen to me closely, Michael. You are embarking on a voyage of discovery. All your previous beliefs will be shaken and challenged. There is nothing to fear if you just remember three rules. One ...

Cut to:

INTERIOR—THE SYBILLINE ORACLE IN ROME

Michael in his Roman officer's uniform. The room still full of fumes. The Oracle dancing and singing.

The dwarfs suddenly emerge from the fumes and seize Michael. He is dragged into deeper fumes and we cannot see him or them.

NEW ANGLE

Amid the fumes, the dwarfs are pushing Michael into some complicated machine which is shaped like the pyramid on the dollar bill.

Cut to:

EXTERIOR: THE CAFE IN CUERNAVACA—
SPECIAL EFFECT

Michael is staring in horror at the pyramids on the American dollar and the Mexican peso. Dwarfs emerge from the pyramids, run around the table, become life-size and drag Michael out of the cafe.

Cathy and Peter do not appear to notice this. Cathy is complaining about Peter's missionary zeal.

CATHY   Dammit, I'm scared. What the hell have you done to my husband?

PETER   Don't worry—he'll be fine ...

Cut to:

INTERIOR—THE SYBILLINE ORACLE

The dwarfs finish pushing Michael into the pyramid-machine. Cut to:

EXTERIOR—MEXICAN DESERT. TRACKING
SHOT.

Michael, wild-eyed, is staggering across a sun-bleached desert toward a huge pyramid. Cut to:

EXTERIOR—MEDIUM CLOSE. TOP OF
PYRAMID

Tree, totally nude, stands atop the pyramid. She looks as enticing and erotic as the Playmate of the Month. She beckons toward Michael invitingly. Cut to:

EXTERIOR TRACKING SHOT—THE MILITARY
FUNERAL

Camera finally moves in close enough for us to recognize Cathy and Michael among the mourners. Her face is streaked with tears. Micheal's face is locked, holding in his grief.

EXTERIOR TRACKING SHOT—THE MEXICAN
DESERT

Michael is climbing the steps of the pyramid toward nude, beautiful Tree. Cut to:

INTERIOR—THE BAR IN CAMBRIDGE.
MEDIUM SHOT.

Michael and Cathy are at a table, and have been celebrating something. The TV is directly above their table and on it we see the final shots of 2001 and hear the familiar World Riddle theme from

Strauss. Michael and Cathy both stop their conversation to look up at the screen for a moment as the Star Child appears and the film ends.

MICHAEL   Well, anyway, as I was saying, I
                           don't believe this parallel universe
                           dogma, even if the whole scientific
                           community stands behind it. One
                           universe is enough for me.

CATHY   Do you know how many Zen Mas-
(*waggish*)   ters it takes to change a light-bulb?

MICHAEL   I'm being serious, dammit. I—hey,
                           that might be a good one. I'll bite.
                           How many Zen Masters *does* it
                           take to change a light-bulb?

CATHY   Two—one to change it and one not
                           to change it.

The TV station above them begins to sign off for the night. On screen appears the Union Jack and voice sings "God Save Our Gracious Queen."

MICHAEL   I get it. One in this universe and one
                           in the universe next door. I still
                           don't believe it. One universe at a
                           time, I say.

CATHY   But if the electrons are in every pos-
                           sible state until we measure them …
                           then every possible universe is real
                           …

Cut to:

EXTERIOR—OUTSIDE THE BAR, CAMBRIDGE
STREET. TRACKING SHOT.

Michael and Cathy are walking toward their car.

MICHAEL (*sarcastic, drunk*)	So we select a possible universe every time we make a sub-atomic measurement? And in the universe next door, I suppose, Washington defeated Arnold and we're not British citizens?
CATHY (*defensive,* *drunk*)	Well, it makes more sense to me than assuming the damned universe really is chaotic and lawless on the quantum level.

We hear the sound of a car skidding.

MICHAEL   The equations don't mean—

A car, out of control, jumps the curb and smashes Cathy against the wall. She screams. It is is obvious that she cannot survive this kind of impact. Michael registers horror and grief. Cut to

INTERIOR—THE ELLIS LIVING ROOM. CLOSE-
UP.

Michael sits dazed in a chair, weeping. Cut to:

NEW ANGLE—MEDIUM SHOT

Michael crossing the room, fighting for control. He climbs the stairs.

MEDIUM SHOT—THE BEDROOM

Michael finds Cathy in bed, alive and asleep. A sob bursts from him and she wakes.

CATHY   What is it, honey? A bad dream?

MICHAEL   There are no words to tell you what
(*hysterical*)   I'm thinking and feeling. Did we
                        win the American Revolution or are
                        we still British?

CATHY   Just hold me, sweetheart. Just hold
                        me.

Michael goes on weeping, unarmored, his body wracked with spasms, as he climbs into the bed and hugs Cathy desperately.

CATHY   It was only a bad dream. Really.
(*soothingly*)   Only a bad dream.

Michael untangles himself from her embrace, sits up.

MICHAEL   Go back to sleep. I'll be all right
                        now. I ... need to walk a bit.

Cathy looks uncertain, but her sleepiness over comes her. She starts to relax back into sleep, then manages one sentence.

CATHY   I love you, Michael.

MICHAEL   I love you, too.

They hold hands for a moment, a grip of long affection. Cathy closes her eyes. Michael waits a moment and then exits.

INTERIOR—CLOSE TRACKING SHOT, THE
LIVING ROOM

Michael in browsing in the bookcase. He finally finds the book he wants and holds it up. We read the title: The Multiple Universe Model in Quantum Physics *by Bryce De Witt, Ph.D.*

He sits and begins reading with absorption. Fade out.

INTERIOR—SIMON'S OFFICE. TRACKING
SHOT.

We pan from a close-up of a fish-tank to a medium shot of Michael and Simon sitting across the desk from each other.

MICHAEL (*a bit nervous still*)   So if I'm not crazy, what am I?

SIMON   You're a man with an allergy to mixing his drugs.

NEW ANGLE

Michael visibly shakes off tension and relaxes more.

MICHAEL   This is *all* just a result of the drugs I had the other day?

SIMON   Maybe. Or the drugs triggered a
                         flashback to the psychedelic mush-
                         rooms In Mexico twenty-five years
                         ago. If that memory was real ...

MICHAEL   I think it was ... if any of my life
                         was real ...

SIMON   We'll come to that. What was the
                         scientific breakthrough you were
                         talking about when you first
                         arrived?

MICHAEL   Well, promise not to decide I'm
(*hesitates*)   crazy after all.... I thought I could
                         check my memories and find proof
                         that parallel universes really exist.

                  NEW ANGLE

Simon rises and feeds the fish in the tank.

SIMON   Would you run that by me again ...
                         a little slower? Remember I'm only
                         a clinical psychologist.

MICHAEL   Most people think it's just science-
                         fiction. So do most physicists.... But
                         there's been a minority for over 20
                         years now who say parallel uni-
                         verses are the simplest explanation
                         of the Schrödinger equations.

Simon resumes his seat.

SIMON   The Schrödinger equations? Can
               you explain that without getting
               too technical?

MICHAEL   The equations seem to give us a
               lawless universe ... an uncertain
               universe. I accept the uncertainty.
               Most physicists do. But some young
               radicals say the uncertainties are
               not just mathematical probabilities
               .... we don't have one lawless uni-
               verse, but an infinite set of lawful
               universes in parallel.

SIMON   I get it ... I think. In one universe
               you took the magic mushrooms, in
               another universe you didn't.

MICHAEL   And in one universe we're British
               citizens and Cathy was killed by a
               car. In this universe, we're Ameri-
               cans and Cathy is alive ...

SIMON   And you think the parapsycholo-
               gists are weird? (*Chuckles.*) Let's
               get out of here and have some air.
               And give Cathy a call. She's proba-
               bly awake by now and getting wor-
               ried.

EXTERIOR—LONG TRACKING SHOT. DAY: A
PARK IN CAMBRIDGE

In the distance we see Michael and Simon walking. On the soundtrack we hear the tune (not the words) of "On A Clear Day You Can See Forever."

EXTERIOR—ANOTHER PART OF THE PARK.
MEDIUM SHOT

Michael and Simon walking. Music of "On a Clear Day" continues.

EXTERIOR—MEDIUM TRACKING SHOT

Michael and Simon walking. Music fades and we begin to hear Simon.

SIMON   Sometimes the most sinister mysteries have the most banal explanations. Back when I was a spook—in Army Intelligence—I spent three months investigating a guy who seemed to be selling stuff to the Russians, or embezzling from the Army, or something nefarious. It turned out he was just cheating on his wife and being super-careful about it.

SAME—LONG TRACKING SHOT

Michael and Simon walking.

SIMON (V.O.)   After breakfast we need to talk to Cathy. She deserves to know ... and maybe she can shed some light on what memories are real ...

*Camera pans rapidly back and moves In close on
the back of a man walking some distance behind
Michael and Simon. The man turns as the path
curves and we recognize him as the man in the car
who has been following Michael. Weird single
musical note.*

*The man slows and is joined by PETER STONE,
20 years older than in Mexico, but youngish and
still hard looking.*

THE MAN   Nothing much. They've been talk-
                     ing half the night.

PETER   I'll take over.

*The man walks off. Peter begins following Michael
and Simon. Camera pans back rapidly. We hear
again hear the tune of "On A Clear Day You Can
See Forever." Slow fade.*

INTERIOR—SIMON'S OFFICE

*Camera pulls back to medium shot and holds. We
see Michael and Cathy, seated in client's chairs, and
Simon, seated behind the desk. Cathy is stunned.
Michael is strained but basically calm.*

SIMON   I have a friend in New York, a psy-
(*concluding*)   chiatrist named Joe Goldfarb, who's
                     treated about—oh—20 or 25 simi-
                     lar cases. Cases involving memories
                     or pseudo-memories of UFO abduc-
                     tion and sexual molestation. Or

genetic tampering. Or whatever it is.

CATHY
(*hesitantly*)

I'm less surprised than I should be.

Pause. *Simon's sympathetic look encourages her to continue.*

CATHY

Michael darling, I always knew there was something... wrong ... (*quick smile*) but not the sort of thing I could write to Ann Landers about ...

MICHAEL

It was just crazy dreams most of my life ... until the dental work and the drugs two days ago.

SIMON

What sort of crazy dreams?

MICHAEL

No UFOs or reincaration.... (*grins*) Parallel universes. In one of them, I'm still here teaching at Harvard but we're not a British colony. This is the Hispanic States of America ...

SIMON (*to Cathy*)

Is it true that a lot of young physicists believe in parallel universes?

CATHY
(*quickly*)

Yes ... and some of them are the brightest young minds around.

NEW ANGLE: CATHY IN FOREGROUND

CATHY	And I find it easier to take than reincarnation ... or midgets from outer space ...
MICHAEL (*tension suddenly showing*)	"I was raped by midgets from Mars!" Christ, what would my friends in the Scientific Skeptics Assocation think? What would the whole fucking faculty think?
SIMON (*joking to relax them*)	It's worse than that. "I killed Christ and then got raped by midgets from Mars."

NEW ANGLE

CATHY	Mike, listen. I'm no psychologist, but I'm sure Simon will agree. If the human mind confronts the literally unthinkable, it invents a screen memory. Isn't that what it's called?
SIMON	Yes. That's what it's called.
CATHY (*to Simon*)	Well, if parallel universes exist, and some minds can sort of travel between them at times; that would be literally unthinkable for most people. Imagine meeting John F. Kennedy in a universe where he never went to Dallas that day. Or seeing paintings by Hitler in a respectable art museum. Screen memories would have to be created to account for the experience.

MICHAEL   There's only one problem with that
(*unsure*)   theory. The parallel universes may
                 be a screen memory for ... *some-*
                 thing else.

Cut to:

INTERIOR—CAL TECH BEDROOM. CLOSE-UP
              ON CATHY

CATHY   ... creatures who claim to be angels
                 may be devils ... demons from
                 hell—trying to enter you—

Cut to:

INTERIOR—SIMON'S OFFICE. NEW ANGLE

Simon in foreground.

SIMON   Let's just consider the Russians for
                 a moment.. Remember Occam's
                 Razor—the simplest possible expla-
                 nation?

Michael and Cathy register surprise and interest.

SIMON   The KGB did have a project, a few
                 years ago, to use psychics to try to
                 influence the minds of Western poli-
                 ticians. That's documented. Maybe
                 they've got another project to work
                 on the minds of Western scientists
                 ...

Cut to:

INTERIOR—HARVARD CLASS-ROOM

Tracking shot shows young Michael listening to lecture and Peter Stone carefully observing Michael. Cut to:

SIMON (V.O.) They may have been working on
        you for years, keeping you under
        surveillance, subtly influencing you
        ...

EXTERIOR—THE CAFE IN CUERNAVACA

Peter is pushing the bag of magic mushrooms across the table to Michael.

INTERIOR—SIMON'S OFFICE. MEDIUM SHOT.

Cathy recovers first.

CATHY   Are you trying to help us or scare
        the shit out of us?

SIMON   A little of both. I want you to be
        fully aware of our total ignorance
        of this type of experience. Your
        ignorance. My ignorance. The igno-
        rance of the whole scientific world.

Simon gets up and begins pacing.

SIMON   Have either of you ever heard of the
        Influencing Machine?

Michael and Cathy shake their heads for "no."

SIMON   There have been papers about in
                        psychological literature for over a
                        century. Certain psychotics, espe-
                        cially schizophrenics, believe in an
                        Influencing Machine which their
                        enemies are using to tamper with
                        their brains. That's how they try to
                        explain their bizarre impressions ...
                        (*Stops by window, turns.*) Descrip-
                        tions of the Influencing Machine, by
                        mental patients, have changed over
                        the decades. It used to be made of
                        gears and levers. Then it got more
                        like a radio. Then it was like TV.
                        Nowadays it's like a modern desk
                        computer ...

CATHY (*warily*)   Simon, what are you getting at?

SIMON   For the last few years I've been
                        thinking about this ... the imagi-
                        nary Influencing Machine invented
                        by the schizophrenics is getting
                        closer and closer to something we
                        actually can duplicate technologi-
                        cally. Their fantasy doesn't sound
                        utterly fantastic anymore.

*He walks to the bookcase and indicates a Neu-
ropep machine.*

SIMON   Here's a device I often use with
                        depressed patients. (*Holding up ear-
                        phones.*) They hear a sound at the
                        low alpha frequency. (*Holding up*

goggles.) And they see a flickering light at the same frequency.

CATHY   Yeah ... I've heard of those gizmos. The patient's brainwaves follow the frequency of the sound and light. They get very relaxed.

SIMON   And mellow. The depression cycle is broken, for a while. But if I turn the frequency even lower, to the delta range, about 70 per cent of all subjects have an "out of body experience"—just as you did two days ago, Mike. Let's not ask how to explain that right now. Just take it as data. They report that they *think* they are outside their body. Usually somewhere near the ceiling ...

CATHY   Aren't there a few dozen of those machines around now?

SIMON   It's a growing market. There's at least 50 brainwave machines around the last time I counted. Most of them are used in hospitals, to treat intractable pain. A few psychologists are experimenting with them, to treat mental problems. But that's just the machines we know about.

Pause. All three exchange glances.

SIMON   I don't see why it wouldn't be possible, theoretically, to program a machine for any kind of brain change you can imagine. Such a machine could even work at a distance, like a parabolic microphone. Point it at some terrorist psycho and he calms down and releases his hostages. Or ... point it at a guy you don't like, change the program, and he gets zapped with hallucinations.

CATHY   They would be Top Secret. Only a few officials would have access to the knowledge. Right, Simon?

Simon crosses the room and sits again.

MICHAEL   Why do I suddenly feel like the Manchurian Candidate?

Ominous note on soundtrack. All look blank, thinking deeply.

SIMON   We're just trying out various lines of interpretation ... we don't *know* anything yet. The Influencing Machine is just another wild guess. I think the two of you should go home and compare memories ... and start phoning old friends for independent verifications when your memories differ. I want to call Joe Goldfarb in New York and see

	if he can fly up here for consultation.
MICHAEL	He's the UFO man?
SIMON	He wouldn't like that description. He's the psychiatrist who's treated a lot of traumatic shock cases where the victims had memories as weird as yours. Including dwarfs who want our sperm—or our chromosomes in the sperm ... for unknown reasons ...

Cut to:

EXTERIOR—STREET OUTSIDE SIMON'S OFFICE. TRACKING SHOT

We see Peter Stone watching Michael and Cathy walk away from Simon's office. One single ominous note, held for 15 seconds. Slow fade.

INTERIOR—ELLIS LIVING ROOM. CLOSE-UP

Cathy is on the phone.

CATHY	Yes ... earthquake activity in Southern California in 1952....

Pan to:

Michael is on another phone.

MICHAEL   Yes, it's wonderful to talk to you
                   again, too, mother.... Look, I want
                   to ask something odd ...

INTERIOR—THE BAR. MEDIUM SHOT

*Michael and Cathy are having a few drinks, but are
not as drunk as in the parallel universe version.
The TV above them is signing off for the night, but
the American flag, not the Union Jack, is flapping
in the breeze.*

CATHY   Well, anyway, the earthquake never
(*continuing a*   happened. Not that night. We
conversation)   found out that much so far.

MICHAEL   But my mother does remember a
                  nut calling me on the phone and
                  pretending to be an extraterrestrial.
                  I hope he *was* just a nut ... (*takes
                  another drink quickly.*)

Tree suddenly walks past their table.

CATHY   Oh, Tree.... Hello!

TREE (*emotions   Oh, Dr. Ellis. *And* Dr. Ellis. Nice to
masked*)   meet again.

MICHAEL (*also   Miss Tree. Good to see you.
masked*)

CATHY   Sit down and have a drink, why
                  don't you?

*Tree and Michael exchange totally enigmatic
glances, very briefly. He has assented.*

TREE (*sitting, next to Cathy*)	Just one. I have a big project I'm working on.
MICHAEL (*easily*)	You know, the night you visited, I never did find out what your field is ...
TREE (*impassive, awaiting his reaction*)	Logic.

NEW ANGLE—MEDIUM CLOSE

MICHAEL (*consternation visible*)	Logic? You're a logic major?
CATHY (*gently*)	Michael ...
MICHAEL	So what's this big project you have to finish tonight?
TREE	I'm not supposed to talk about it.... but, well, it's about people who aren't crazy but see things that sound crazy. It's for Dr. Selene and a friend of his named Dr. Goldfarb.

Now Michael and Cathy exchange masked glances.

MICHAEL	Joe Goldfarb ... yes, Simon has mentioned him. He's the guy who treats UFO witnesses with trauma ... Right?

TREE   I shouldn't say anymore. The gov-
                        ernment may be involved.

*Camera pans back. We see a man put some money
in the jukebox. Camera moves back in on table.*

TREE   So what are you two working on
                        lately? Not more bombs, I hope.

MICHAEL   We've been investigating the theo-
(*easily*)   retical implications of the parallel
                        universe theory. Every electron is
                        literally in every possible state,
                        somewhere in super-space ...

*The juke box blares out "On a Clear Day You can
See Forever," this time with lyrics as well as just the
music. Michael stops, entranced. Camera pans
slowly around the table as Michael, Cathy and
Tree each show a strong emotional reaction to the
words.*

LYRIC   On a clear day, rise and look
                        around you,

                        And you'll see who you are

                        On a clear day, it will astound you

                        How the glow of your being out-
                        shines every star ...

*Close up on Michael, showing simple awe and
uncertainty.*

MICHAEL   I'm the man who's not crazy but
(*suddenly*)   has been seeing crazy things. The

one that got Simon interested in this
project.

Now Tree looks absolutely astonished.

TREE   You! I thought you were the type
                      who'd block that kind of perception
                      ... turn it off....

MICHAEL   I did, for years and years.... but it
                      finally caught up with me ...

Pause. We hear the jukebox again.

JUKEBOX   On a clear day you can see forever
                      ... and ever ... and ever more ...

Fade.

EXTERIOR NIGHT—THE STREET OUTSIDE THE
BAR

*This is exactly the scene we saw before, except that
Tree is present.*

CATHY (*with   So Schrödinger proved the cat was
humor*)   dead and alive at the same time. But
                      so am I. And so are you ... in differ-
                      ent universes ...

We hear the car approaching.

MICHAEL (*also   And if you consider the genetics of
feeling witty*)   conception ... everybody born male
                      in one universe is born female in
                      another universe. And every woman
                      here is a man in some other world.

> Can you imagine Hugh Hefner as a woman?

We hear the car skidding and it shoots up onto the sidewalk. Michael grabs Cathy and pulls her back. Tree jumps back on her own. The car smashes into the wall, hitting none of them.

CLOSE-UP—MICHAEL

MICHAEL   Cathy just died in the universe next
(*stunned*)   door.

Tree and Cathy stare at him. Slow fade.

INTERIOR NIGHT CLOSE SHOT—THE ELLIS
BEDROOM

Cathy is sleeping soundly. Michael tosses restlessly in his sleep. Camera pans in and he speaks in his dream.

MICHAEL (*in   Charlie ...
anguish*)

LONG SHOT DAY EXTERIOR—THE BEACH

Cathy and Michael and their son, in bathing suits, running happily.

CLOSE UP—MICHAEL IN BED

He moans in grief.

MEDIUM SHOT—THE ELLIS KITCHEN

Michael is making coffee. The boy, Charlie, aged about 3, is examining a can opener.

CHARLIE   Know why is called can opener?
(*happy with
himself*)

MICHAEL   Well, no, Charlie. You tell me why.
(*affectionate*)

CHARLIE   Because why. Because *can open!*
(*proudly*)

Michael registers delight. He hugs the boy.

MICHAEL   Bright as a penny you are. Bright as
                   a penny.

MEDIUM SHOT—ELLIS LIVING ROOM

*A young man, Charlie at about 20, speaks directly
to the camera, sincerely*

CHARLIE   I know I can get a deferment to con-
                   tinue my studies, but I love this
                   country, Dad. It's my duty to serve.

REPEAT SHOT—HARVARD YARD

The chanting student radicals.

STUDENTS   One! Two! Three! Four! We don't
                   want your fucking war!

CLOSE UP—FRONT PAGE OF NEWSPAPER

Photo of Charlie in uniform. Headline:

CHARLES ELLIS KILLED IN ACTION

Smaller type:

SON OF TWO HARVARD SCIENTISTS

TRACKING SHOT—THE FUNERAL

We hear "Taps" mournfully played. Camera moves in slowly, very slowly, on Cathy as she weeps more and more hysterically. Eventually the sound of her weeping drowns out the mournful music of "Taps."

Pan to Michael. His face is dead, all emotion gone. Cathy's weeping continues as he registers nothing at all.

LONG SHOT—OUTSIDE THE ELLIS HOUSE

Various mourners are trying to make helpful and consoling remarks. Cathy is trying to be grateful to them. Michael looks like a zombie.

MEDIUM SHOT—THE BEDROOM

Cathy lies sprawled on the bed, weeping again. Michael is sitting, rubbing her shoulders tenderly.

LONG SHOT—THE BEDROOM

We see twilight through the window. Cathy is asleep. Michael rises and walks from the room.

MEDIUM SHOT—THE LIVING ROOM

Michael walks stiffly to one of the walls. He takes down a plaque commemorating some scientific award he has won. He begins coldly and methodically smashing it against the corner of the desk. His rage rises slowly and he smashes the pieces into pieces, gasping and panting. A sound emerges from his lips—not grief, but rage. He smashes the plaque again and again.

MEDIUM SHOT—THE BEDROOM

Michael tossing in the bed, Cathy sleeping beside him. Charlie appears, without uniform, in casual civilian dress, near the door.

CHARLIE   Don't, Dad. Don't mourn. I am always.

MICHAEL   Charlie.... Is it possible?
(*talking in his
sleep*)

CHARLIE   I am always. We are all ... always
                   ...

Charlie fades. Michael sinks into deeper, dreamless sleep. Fade to:

INTERIOR MEDIUM SHOT—SIMON'S OFFICE

Simon is sitting behind his desk. In an easy chair nearby is a midget. Michael and Cathy enter. Simon rises.

SIMON   Dr. Mike Ellis and Dr. Cathy Ellis. My old friend, Dr. Joe Goldfarb.

Michael is visibly suprised.

GOLDFARB   Simon didn't tell you I was a
                  midget?

MICHAEL   I ... uh ...

GOLDFARB   You'll get used to it. I have. I've
(*imperturbable*) even found that it helps me in ther-
                  apy. Especially with depressives.
                  They end up feeling sorry for *me*.
                  You'd be astounded at what an
                  improvement that is. Most neurot-
                  ics never feel sorry for anyone but
                  themselves.

MEDIUM TRACKING SHOT—NEW ANGLE

GOLDFARB   Have you heard of the GCSI?

MICHAEL   No ...

GOLDFARB   I invented it. Hasn't come into
                  widespread use yet, but that's
                  because my colleagues are mostly
                  ass-holes. Shall I impart my wisdom
                  to you?

SIMON   I've never found a way of stopping
(*smiling*)   you, Joe.

CLOSE-UP: GOLDFARB

GOLDFARB   The GCSI is the Goldfarb Cosmic
                  Schmuck Inventory. Named after its
                  inventor. No false modesty. Simon,

can you think of three times you've
acted like a Cosmic Schmuck this
week?

TRACKING SHOT AROUND THE ROOM

SIMON	I can think of ten times at least.
GOLDFARB	Good, good. Then you're not totally a Cosmic Schmuck. How about you, Michael?
MICHAEL	I've been a Cosmic Shmuck *all* week.
GOLDFARB	Fine. Cathy?
CATHY (*smiling*)	Well, at least three times.
GOLDFARB	Wonderful, a room full of people who are recovering from the Number One Plague of the human race, Cosmic Schmuckery. Do you know why most people *never* recover? Because they never admit they have been acting like Cosmic Shmucks. They're afraid they'll lose face. So they go on acting like Cosmic Shmucks forever.

Michael sits down wearily.

MICHAEL	Four days ago I was in that category. I would never, never admit I was wrong about anything.

NEW ANGLE

GOLDFARB   Yes, Simon has filled me in on your
                 case. Would it surprise you to know
                 I've treated exactly 32 men and
                 women who believe they've had
                 their genitals molested by bald-
                 headed extraterrestrials?

*A single weird, high note on the soundtrack.
Everybody glances at everybody else. Michael visibly struggles for control.*

MICHAEL   Simon told me you had some back-
                 ground in this sort of thing ... trau-
                 matic shock ...

GOLDFARB   Simon said what you were ready to
                 hear. You've had another day to
                 mull it over. You can stand more of
                 the truth. Traumatic shock is only
                 part of the answer.

MICHAEL   Okay. I'm braced. Tell me.

GOLDFARB   "Hallucination" is just not an ade-
                 quate word for your experience.
                 Call it rapid brain change. It's an
                 opportunity to learn a million new
                 things very fast.

MICHAEL   All I've learned so far is the wide ...
                 large ... deep ... almost infinite
                 extent of my own ignorance.

GOLDFARB   You stopped being a Cosmic Sch-
                 muck who doesn't know it and
                 became a Cosmic Schmuck who
                 does know it. Socrates considered
                 that the beginning of wisdom. But
                 you've learned more than that,
                 really. Think about it.

MICHAEL   I've learned that I have more doubts
                 about nuclear research than I ever
                 admitted to myself. 30 years ago I
                 stopped saying things that might
                 threaten my Security Clearance.
                 Then, gradually, I even stopped
                 thinking such things. I lost part of
                 myself ...

There is a knock. Simon rises and opens the door.

MEDIUM CLOSE—THE DOORWAY

*Tree is standing in the door, with a large computer
graphic print-out. She is conservatively dressed for
once, but still overwhelming.*

TREE   Oh, hello, Cathy ... Mike ...

SIMON   Come in. Mike and Cathy are part
                 of our research team now. And this
                 is Joe Goldfarb from New York.

*Tree crosses the room. Every man's eyes follow her.
She hangs her chart from a corner of the bookcase.*

TREE   Simon, I know Mike is your uh sub-
                 ject. He told me last night.

Quick exchange of glances between Simon and Michael. Cathy catches this and looks puzzled.

TREE *(trying to cover)*   I met Mike and Cathy at a bar. They told me about Mike's ... visions. Anyway, here's a logical flow chart of the possiblities. I used Venn diagrams.

Camera pans to the logical chart which looks like an avalanche of circles, some inside others, some totally distinct from all others, some overlapping.

TREE   Over here, we have the totally subjective theories ... hallucination or trauma. I've divided it into psychological, like Freudian or Jungian, and physiological, like earthquakes or car accidents or the drugs Mike got from you and the dentist.... Then here we have the objective theories ... real extraterrestrials, or some conspiracy that's doing it and faking the extraterrestrials, or parallel universes, or bilocation in time, bilocation in space, and so on ... and way over here is God and Miracles. Somebody who couldn't deal with religious experience might create all the other frames to protect himself from ah well *(smiles)* the hand of God trying to influence him ...

MICHAEL   It's ... philosophical spaghetti....
                           We'll never disentangle it. My God,
                           more than half the circles overlap.

TREE   In pure logic I had to do that. More
                           than one of these theories may be
                           true at the same time.

SIMON   Extraterrestrials and Russians
(*pointing*)   working together.... You thought of
                           that one yourself, Mike.

CATHY   But that overlap there.... *God* and
(*putting on her*   the Russians?
glasses*)

                    MEDIUM SHOT—THE ROOM

SIMON   Start here, with the Russians. Either
                           they have contact with extraterres-
                           trials or they're faking it. Both
                           bridges lead down here—they can
                           control minds with some unknown
                           technology.

CATHY   You've treated a couple of dozen of
                           these cases, Joe ... but how many
                           would you say there are in the
                           country as a whole?

GOLDFARB   I'd be guessing.... Most of the peo-
                           ple who've been on this roller-
                           coaster don't want to talk about it
                           all ... what has gotten onto the
                           mass media, or even into the shlock

152 ROBERT ANTON WILSON

tabloids, may be just the tip of the
iceberg. There may be millions.

MICHAEL   What the hell do you really think,
Joe?

MEDIUM CLOSE ON GOLDFARB

GOLDFARB   I read once about a Cockney fish
(*carefully*)   peddlar who had a vision of God....
He went around telling everybody,
"God is just as lovely as a barrel of
apples."

CATHY   That was the only image he had for
(*touched*)   beauty ...

GOLDFARB   We psychiatrists know that the conscious ego is just a conditioned
mechanism, like a rat in a laboratory ... the true self is something
much bigger ... and we don't know
how much bigger.... Maybe the
Orient is right and the true self is
the whole universe, past and
present and future, and all of the
space-time continuum.

MEDIUM SHOT—MICHAEL, CATHY AND TREE

TREE (*her*   Michael, what he's saying is that
affection   mystical experience can happen to
showing)   anybody.... If you're an Atheist, it
won't look like God, but It will
shake you and bend you just like

the Hand of God until you have
been reborn into a new kind of person. Don't you see?

Pan to close-up on Cathy. She observes Tree's affectionate tone, and suddenly she registers—we see that she knows, intuitively, that Mike and Tree have been lovers. Her face hardens.

MICHAEL   I wonder ... could it be that simple,
                 really? No parallel universes or rap-
                 ists from space, no sinister Russians
                 ...

NEW ANGLE—MEDIUM SHOT

GOLDFARB   It's not simple at all. You have a lot
                  of emotions and ideas to process—
                  emotions and ideas you've been
                  afraid to look at for years or
                  decades. (*Flat. direct. clinical:*)
                  Simon tells me you lost a son in
                  Vietnam. He doesn't appear at all in
                  your visions. You're still repressing
                  grief ... and God knows what else
                  connected with Vietnam ...

MICHAEL   I saw Charlie last night. In a dream.
(*simply*)   He was in heaven. I don't even
                  believe in heaven, but it made me
                  feel better.

Cathy registers sympathy, but still looks angry about Michael and Tree.

GOLDFARB   The unconscious is more merciful
                  and less critical than our blasted
                  over-educated egos. If you can't
                  believe in heaven while you're
                  awake, you can believe it while
                  you're asleep. That's part of the
                  healing.

*Camera pans back slowly. Michael is beginning to
register acceptance and the ability to endure the
Mystery. Simon clears his throat and camera moves
to angle featuring him as center.*

SIMON   As a psychologist, I agree totally
                  with my eminent colleague from
                  New York. As a former spook, I
                  have to tell you all there's more to
                  this than psychology ...

                  NEW ANGLE

SIMON   You never forget that training. I
                  walk down a street and notice tat-
                  toos or other identifying marks. I
                  look at windows to see if an assas-
                  sin up there would get a good shot
                  at a motorcade ...

CATHY   What are you telling us?

SIMON   I know I've been under surveillance
                  for three days. I suspect that Mike
                  has a tail, too. I'm damned sure it
                  started when he first came to me
                  with this story.

CATHY

It may not be connected with this at all. They may do random checks once or twice a year ...

GOLDFARB

I do not believe in coincidences. I'll tell you what it is. We have asked the wrong questions. We have breached National Security. We're in the shit, all of us.

MICHAEL

Now let's not go postal.... I think anybody with my kind of Clearance undergoes periodic surveillance ...

SIMON

Well, we don't have to get stone paranoid about a few spooks.... It's just another factor to consider ...

The doors smash open. Four men in black suits enter. Two are Peter Stone and the man who has been following Michael. The other two are new to us.

PETER
(*showing badge*)

U.S. Marshal. I must ask you all to come with us.

CLOSE UP—CATHY

CATHY (*with total terror*)

Oh, my Christ ... it's going to be worse than anything we guessed ...

Quick blackout. Silence. Blank screen indicates passage of time.

LONG SHOT INTERIOR—BETWEEN TWO BARE
WHITE WALLS

Michael is being escorted or dragged down the hall by Peter Stone and another agent.

MICHAEL   I'm a loyal citizen ... an important scientist ...

PETER   We're your government. We just want to protect you. The voters elected us.

They come to a bare white door in the bare white hall. Michael is ushered in. The two agents stay outside and slam the door hard. Pause. Then we hear a terrible scream. Blackout. Pause to indicate time passing.

INTERIOR—RECEPTION AREA OF PSYCHIATRIC HOSPITAL

Michael stands listlessly between two orderlies. He looks drugged or catatonic. Nurse is writing.

FIRST   Smith, James. Looks catatonic. Put
ORDERLY   him in the Special Ward.

INTERIOR—LONG TRACKING SHOT BETWEEN ROWS OF CABINETS

Camera zooms down an almost endless row of cabinets and comes to a robot-like servo mechanism, which opens a drawer and removes a file. The "hand" or claw of the robot pulls out a photo of Michael Ellis. Another mechanical device descends upon the photo. As the device moves back we see the photo is marked RESIGNED.

INTERIOR—LONG LIBRARY-LIKE ROOM.

The Board of Directors of Harvard are meeting.

PRESIDENT   Next item on the agenda. Dr. Ellis of our physics department has had to move West for reasons of health. I vote that we send him a gold watch as a token of our esteem, for all his good work these many years.

BOARD   Second.
MEMBER

PRESIDENT   Any opposition? So moved.

Blackout. Pause to indicate time passing.

INTERIOR—LARGE AUDITORIUM (SAME AS PREVIOUS S.S.A. MEETING). MEDIUM LONG SHOT

More or less the same group of white middle-aged male scientists as before, but Carl now appears to be an officer. Peter Stone is sitting next to him.

CARL   Dr. Ellis, who had to move to Arizona for health reasons, has written us asking to be relieved of all duties as Vice President of the Scientific Skeptics Association. I would like to nominate Peter Stone to take up Dr. Ellis's job.

ELDERLY   Second.
MEMBER

SIMON (*V.O.*)   Let me speak, damn it.

MEDIUM CLOSE SHOT—BACK OF
AUDITORIUM

Simon is struggling with two Ushers.

SIMON   I want to talk to the press. This
whole thing is a fraud. They're all
working for the CIA—

PETER STONE   Please remove that disturbed indi-
(*V.O.*)   vidual gently.

SIMON   They made some dirty deal with the
extraterrestrials way back in the
1940s and they've been hiding it
from us ever since. They killed
Kennedy when he found out ...

*Simon is dragged out. A few reporters look with
amusement at the "madman."*

SIMON   I'm not crazy, damn it. I'm a psychologist myself ... I know ... I saw
... I was a witness ...

Camera pans to medium close shot of the podium

CARL (*to press*)   That poor man has been ill for two
years now.... Please don't write
anything about this ... it would
embarass his family.

Blackout. Pause to indicate time passing.

INTERIOR—PSYCHIATRIC WARD

Michael, in cheap hospital gown, walks among demented and dazed fellow patients. Suddenly from another ward we hear a totally mad laugh, rising louder and more shrill for a while, then choked off.

MICHAEL
(V.O.,
remembering)

"At the bottom of Hell are the stairs of Paradise."

Blackout. Pause to indicate time passing.

EXTERIOR—LONG SHOT, THE ELLIS HOUSE, WINTER

Snow is falling and we hear the tune of "Silent Night." A car drives into the driveway and Cathy gets out. She looks greyer and has more lines in her face. She unloads two heavy packages. The door opens and an attractive middle aged man comes out to help her with the packages. He is either her new husband or new lover.

INTERIOR—THE ELLIS LIVING ROOM

Michael's Star Trek *poster has disappeared and there are a few bits of African sculpture. Otherwise it is as bookish and untidy as ever.*

CATHY

Tom, be an angel ... make me a very dry martini.

She sits and starts to remove her galoshes. Tom exits to kitchen. Cathy sighs with exhaustion. Phone rings. She picks it up.

CATHY   Who? No, goddam it, I don't want
                     to talk to you.

INTERIOR—MAGAZINE OFFICE

*Sign identifies UFO JOURNAL. A dozen sketches
of bald-headed dwarfs by various Contactees are
hung on the walls. There are slight differences but
basically they all look alike.*

JOURNALIST   I just want a few moments of your
                     time. The rumors about your hus-
                     band and the UFOnauts are being
                     published in lots of sensational
                     newspapers. We try to be honest
                     here. We want the facts.

INTERIOR—THE ELLIS LIVING ROOM

CATHY   In the first place, he's my ex-hus-
                     band. The last I heard from him
                     was over three years ago. He was in
                     a hospital in New Mexico or Ari-
                     zona or somewhere. There's noth-
                     ing else to tell. Please please please
                     Please leave me alone. (*Hangs up
                     violently.*)

Tom enters with two martinis.

TOM   The yellow press again?

CATHY   Oh, Jesus, Tom.... We're going to
                     have to change our phone number
                     again. I can't take this.

TOM (*kissing her*)	Why not just unplug it till after Christmas? I can get the number changed then.
CATHY	You're an angel.... Jesus, it's bad enough to have your husband go bananas, the guy you lived with for 30 years ... raving and ranting and smashing the furniture ... (*she obviously "remembers" events this way now*) but then the ghouls keep haunting you years and years after ...

Tom unplugs phone.

TOM (*kissing her again*)	There, there ... it will be all right ...

Slow fade to blackout. Pause.

EXTERIOR LONG SHOT—PARK AVENUE, NEW YORK

Traffic. We pan in on one high window.

INTERIOR—DR. GOLDFARB'S OFFICE

Dr. Goldfarb is looking out the window and stretching. He turns and buzzes the intercom.

GOLDFARB	Next patient.

The door opens and a nervous, obese man enters. He is startled that Goldfarb is a midget.

GOLDFARB   Have a seat, Mr ... (*looks at card*) Moriarity. What can I do for you?

MEDIUM CLOSE SHOT—MORIARITY AND GOLDFARB

MORIARITY   I uh heard that you deal with uh unusual cases ... people who have seen uh strange things.

GOLDFARB   What sort of strange things do you
(*carefully*)   have in mind?

MORIARITY   I saw something ... people would say I was crazy.... I'm not sure ... Doctor, I think I saw extraterrestri- als in a field doing something awful to cattle ...

GOLDFARB   I don't handle cases of that sort
(*briskly*)   anymore. I'll write the name and phone number of a doctor who is very good with that kind of prob- lem. (*Writing.*) Psychiatry has come a long way, Mr. Moriarity ... the right chemicals will have you back to normal in a comparatively short time ...

Moriarity looks downcast. Slow fade.

LONG SHOT FROM HELICOPTER—DAY, EXTERIOR

We are looking down at a religious commune somewhere in the hills of perhaps Oregon or

Northern California. As camera pans lower we see various robed men and women working in the gardens.

INTERIOR LONG SHOT—MEDITATION HALL

We pan between two rows of students meditating and find Tree among them. A gong sounds. The students start to rise.

MEDIUM LONG SHOT—THE GROUNDS

Tree and a young male student are walking and talking.

MALE

I heard that you once worked for Dr. Selene, the crazy guy.

TREE

Yes. Poor Simon.

MALE

What went wrong with him?

TREE

He saw the Face of God and wasn't ready.

MALE

But how could Dr. Selene see God and come away raving about evil extraterrestrials and CIA assassins and all that?

TREE

In the Dark Ages, monks who opened the curtain too soon started raving about demons and devils. Extraterrestrials and CIA agents are just our modern demons. Until the mind is free of fear—completely

free—every Cosmic Mind manifes-
tation appears as something threat-
ening and terrible ...

MALE   My God ...

TREE   Well, now you know why most people never raise the curtain.... They
couldn't bear what they would see
...

EXTERIOR—GROUNDS OF A MENTAL
HOSPITAL. TRACKING SHOT

Close-up shows Michael, whiter in the beard, hap-
pily working in the garden. As camera pans back,
two psychiatrists enter the frame.

PSYCHIATRIST   James here is doing very well. We
#1 (*to Psychia-*   may release him soon.
trist #2)

Camera continues to dolly back and up. Psychia-
trists walk off and Michael returns to his garden-
ing. Camera pulls far back and up and we see that
he has turned the whole garden into a giant peace
symbol when seen from the sky. Slow fade.

INTERIOR: THE TV STUDIO—CLOSE UP

We see the same TV Host we saw earlier.

TV HOST   And now tonight our long-awaited
UFO debate ... with the leading
authorities representing all the leading viewpoints. First, on the right,

let me present Dr. Carl Martin of the Scientific Skeptics Assocation. Dr. Martin?

Camera pans back. We see Carl and Simon and two others on the panel.

CARL

My position is simple. There is no UFO mystery at all. Every sighting we have investigated is just an ordinary object—a weather balloon or a helicopter with bright lights at night—or else the witnesses are people trying to make money out of a deliberate fraud.

TV HOST

Strong words. This should be a lively night. Mr. Petrie?

NEW ANGLE

MR. PETRIE

Dr. Martin is just expressing opinions. I know the facts. I was aboard a UFO for three hours. The Space Brothers are far more advanced than us and they have come here to save this planet from human greed, ecological disaster and nuclear war. We must greet them with love ...

TV HOST

We'll hear more of that later, folks. Dr. Kirk?

DR. KIRK

Nobody knows what UFOs are. I've been studying them for 30 years

and I know less than when I started.
People who want easy answers,
invent easy answers for themselves.
If you want the truth, as I do, you
find that there are no easy answers.
They are not spaceships. They are
not hallucinations. They are nothing we can understand with
present-day science.

TV HOST   Maybe my mother-in-law is one of
                          them.... Science can't explain her....
                          Dr. Selene?

SIMON (*with*   They're extraterrestrials all right,
the glare of the   and Dr. Martin knows it. The CIA
True Paranoid)   has known it since the 1940s and
                          Dr. Martin's group is just a CIA
                          front. Our government made a deal
                          with them—the Space creatures—
                          back in the 1940s. The National
                          Security Act of 1948 had nothing to
                          do with the Cold War ...

INTERIOR NIGHT—A BAR IN DETROIT

*Camera pans back and we see people at the bar
watching the TV.*

SIMON   The Cold War itself is a giant decep-
(*continued*)   tion. National Security is a mask to
                          allow the government to hide and
                          conceal everything it wants to keep
                          from us—all the details of how

they're selling us out to the extraterrestrials ... enslaving us ...

MAN AT BAR   Hey, this guy might be right ... I heard about a UFO that crashed in 1948 ...

WOMAN   Jesus, Pete, don't scare me. I don't
WITH MAN   wanna think about that.

Camera continues to pan down bar.

CARL   Dr. Selene makes reckless charges wherever he appears ... charges without a shred of evidence ...

MR PETRIE   He's been hypnotized by the demons of the lower astral. The Space Brothers worship the same God as us and act as His messengers ... Jesus was a Space Brother ...

CARL   Dr. Selene had to be retired from Harvard because of mental instability ...

SIMON   You and your friends in the CIA framed me ...

Camera pans to a man in a leather jacket. He pays his bill and turns. It is Michael Ellis. His beard is snowy white and he looks serene.

BARTENDER   Leaving already, Adam?

MICHAEL   Gotta get back to work.

EXTERIOR NIGHT—OUTSIDE THE BAR

A cab stands by the curb. Michael gets in and takes the driver's seat. He looks around. A woman rushes to the door, waving. He opens for her.

INTERIOR—THE CAB IS MOVING

MICHAEL   Where to, lady?

The woman is about 35, good-looking, very worried.

WOMAN   St. John's Hospital.

MICHAEL   Nothing serious, I hope?

WOMAN   My husband.... He had a heart
                 attack today ...

MICHAEL   You know, lady ... I get hunches
                 sometimes.... My friends tell me
                 I'm psychic. I think your husband's
                 going to be all right.

CLOSE-UP OF THE WOMAN

WOMAN   Thanks, mister. I wish I could
                 believe you.

CLOSE-UP OF MICHAEL

MICHAEL   Mrs. Bukowski, you *can* believe me.
(*with total
Authority*)

LONG SHOT—EXTERIOR OF HOSPITAL

The cab pulls up to the entrance.

MEDIUM SHOT—INSIDE CAB

WOMAN   Hey, how did you know my name?
(*passing Michael
a bill*)

MICHAEL   Like I said, I get hunches sometimes
                         ...

EXTERIOR NIGHT LONG SHOT

The woman gets out of the cab, looking more confident. The cab shoots away at once. She looks at her hand in astonishment.

WOMAN   Hey, you made a mistake.... You
(*shouting after   gave me a hundred dollar bill in the
the cab*)   change ...

EXTERIOR NIGHT LONG SHOT—STREET CORNER IN DETROIT

A man comes out of a pool room. The cab pulls up near him.

MICHAEL   Hey, Nathan!

NATHAN   Jesus, it's the Golden Boy again.

MEDIUM SHOT

Nathan leans into the cab and hands Mike a wad of money.

NATHAN

I don't know how you do it....
Everybody thought that dog would
still be running when the next race
started.

MICHAEL
(*easily*)

I get hunches.

NATHAN

Well, Mr. Anthropos, you're a nice
guy, but I wish you'd take your
business to another bookie. You're
bankrupting me. I get a hernia carrying your winnings around all day
waiting to see you.

MICHAEL
(*seriously*)

I only bet when I need the money.

NATHAN

Christ, I hope you don't need a lot
of money one of these weeks.

EXTERIOR LONG SHOT—DAWN

*Michael parks his cab in front of a cheap boarding
house.*

MEDIUM SHOT—EXTERIOR STAIRWAY OF
BOARDING HOUSE

*Michael is walking up the stairs. A black man
appears below him on the street.*

BLACK MAN

Are you Adam Anthropos?

MICHAEL

That's my name. Are you in trouble,
Mr. ... uh ...

BLACK MAN   George Bridge. Can I come up and
                   talk to you?

MICHAEL   My reputation is spreading....
                   Come on in.

INTERIOR—CHEAP ROOM, VERY CLEAN BUT
OLD AND POOR

Michael is making coffee. George sits nervously.

MICHAEL   Tell me about it.

GEORGE   They say you work miracles.

MICHAEL   No ... I show people how to work
                   their own miracles. Tell me,
                   George—what do you need?

GEORGE   It's my baby. She's only six.... The
                   doctor says she's got the leukemia.
                   She won't live a year, he says.

*Michael sets down two cups of coffee and joins
George at the table.*

MICHAEL   Doctors don't know everything.
                   Drink your coffee.

Pause while both sip.

MICHAEL   Do you know who runs the Crack
                   trade around here?

GEORGE   What you care about that? Who are
(*suspicious,*   you?
almost paranoid)

MICHAEL   Suppose you knew a man in that
               business ... I know where he can get
               an honest job. It won't pay as
               much, but I guarantee he won't get
               shot by a rival gang and he won't
               go to jail.

GEORGE (*in   Motherfuck.... You are just what
awe*)   they told me. Man, you sayin' I
               gotta give up dealing Crack before
               you help me?

MICHAEL   No, I don't make conditions. Some-
               times I just offer more than I'm
               asked for. I get hunches ... I think
               you might be found dead in a few
               days if you don't get out of the
               Crack business.

GEORGE   How about my baby?

MICHAEL   She's okay. Believe me. The doctor
               will tell you by this afternoon. He'll
               call it spontaneous remission.

GEORGE   What kind of money you get for
               this?

MICHAEL   Nothing. I get my money ... other
               ways.... (*Writing:*) Here's the name
               and address. Go see about that job.

George looks at him for a long time, wondering.

GEORGE   My man, don't worry about our
               high crime rate. My baby lives like

you say, and I put the word out.
Nobody will ever lay a hand on
you.

MICHAEL   Thank you. The word is already
out. I have many ... clients.

George leaves, with a profound nod of respect. Michael finishes his coffee and takes both cups to the sink. He walks behind the bed and we see a meditation cushion. Michael sits in the classic lotus position and goes into deep meditation at once.

LONG TRACKING SHOT

An American Indian shaman. He looks up and grins.

MEDIUM SHOT

An aged Rabbi somewhere in Israel. He looks up and smiles.

CLOSE UP

Michael meditating and smiling. The first notes of "Ode to Joy."

SPECIAL EFFECT

The faces of Michael, the shaman and the Rabbi all smiling, all obviously in communication.

New faces come into the montage—an African shaman, an Arabic Sufi, a Buddhist monk, a house-wife in a small American town, Dr. Abraham

Baum, an English fish peddlar, then dozens of ordinary faces from around the world including Latin Americans, Frenchmen, Italians, more Orientals, etc. "Ode to Joy" grows louder.

Tree's face suddenly emerges from the montage and she seems to recognize Michael. She smiles radiantly.

A panorama of children's faces. All are between six and nine and they represent every race and nation on the planet. All are smiling in a knowing and blissful way.

"Ode to Joy" races toward its climax as the faces of the children form a spiral. The spiral gradually fades into the spiral of the galaxy.

Among billions of stars we hear the last bars of Beethoven's hymn to peace and to the unity of all living beings.

Other Books By Robert Anton Wilson

*Published by New Falcon Publications

WHAT CRITICS SAY ABOUT
ROBERT ANTON WILSON

A **SUPER-GENIUS**...He has written everything I was afraid to write
— Dr. John Lilly

One of the funniest, most incisive social critics around, and with a
positive bent, thank Goddess.
— Riane Eisler, author of *The Chalice and the Blade*

A very funny man...readers with open minds will like his books.
— Robin Robertson, *Psychological Perspectives*

Robert Anton Wilson is a dazzling barker hawking tickets to the most
thrilling tilt-a-whirls and daring loop-o-planes on the midway of higher
consciousness.
— Tom Robbins, author of *Even Cowgirls Get the Blues*

OBSCENE, blasphemous, subversive and very, very interesting.
— Alan Watts

Erudite, witty and genuinely scary.
— PUBLISHER'S WEEKLY

STUPID
— Andrea Antonoff

A 21st Century Renaissance Man...funny, wise and optimistic...
— DENVER POST

The world's greatest writer-philosopher.
— IRISH TIMES (Dublin)

Hilarious...multi-dimensional...a laugh a paragraph.
— LOS ANGELES TIMES

Ranting and raving...negativism...
— Neal Wilgus

**One of the most important writers working in English
today**...courageous, compassionate, optimistic and original.
— Elwyn Chamberling, author of *Gates of Fire*

Should win the Nobel Prize for INTELLIGENCE.
— QUICKSILVER MESSENGER (Brighton, England)